CHRISTIAN BIBLE CHALLENGE

ANSWERS EVERY CHRISTIAN SHOULD KNOW

What is Christianity?
What is the primary topic of the Bible?
What is the grand theme of the Bible?
How does Christianity differ from religions of men?

Question & Answer Format

Jerry Adams
Bible Student and Teacher

In the Year of Our Lord 2013

CHRISTIAN BIBLE CHALLENGE

ANSWERS EVERY CHRISTIAN SHOULD KNOW

WestBow
PRESS
A DIVISION OF THOMAS NELSON

WestBow Press books may be ordered through booksellers or by contacting:

WestBow Press
A Division of Thomas Nelson
1663 Liberty Drive
Bloomington, IN 47403
www.westbowpress.com
1-(866) 928-1240

Because of the dynamic nature of the Internet, any web addresses or links contained in this book may have changed since publication and may no longer be valid. The views expressed in this work are solely those of the author and do not necessarily reflect the views of the publisher, and the publisher hereby disclaims any responsibility for them.

Any people depicted in stock imagery provided by Thinkstock are models, and such images are being used for illustrative purposes only.

Certain stock imagery © Thinkstock.

ISBN: 978-1-4497-9237-4 (sc)
ISBN: 978-1-4497-9259-6 (e)

Library of Congress Control Number: 2013907304

Printed in the United States of America.

WestBow Press rev. date: 05/09/2013

To my family,
and to those who have participated with me in Bible studies and posed questions.
You inspired me to write this book.

FOREWORD

The greatest American freedom is freedom of worship. We are free to read and interpret the Bible for ourselves. Only a handful of us do. Forty percent who claim to be Christians cannot name the four Gospels. An even greater percentage cannot name more than five of the Ten Commandments.

For centuries millions of confessing Christians were actually forbidden to read or interpret the Bible for themselves. They were told they were not trained and not qualified. Many preachers in various denominations pretended they were the only ones who could tell their congregations what the Bible really meant. In a sense there was almost a conspiracy to prevent us from knowing the Word of God for ourselves.

No one can know the Word of God for you. Whatever your question, your doubt, your struggles – as a believer in Jesus Christ, you need to know what God says.

In our nation we delegate anything that can be delegated. That includes knowing the Word of God. It cannot be delegated to others – not to their sermons, denominations, Christian books, Internet, TV or radio programs. All these are helps, but what good is the answer if you do not know it **for yourself** from the **Word of God**?

How do you evaluate what you hear or read as to whether it confirms or undermines God's Word? The only standard for a Christian is the Word of God in the Bible. A wonderful church is never a substitute for the believer **personally studying** and **personally interpreting** the Word of God **for himself**.

For more than 31 years Jerry Adams has taught Bible classes. He has seen the famine from which most American Christians suffer – no **personal** knowledge of what God says. Jerry is insistent that every Christian has to know for himself what the Word of God says.

"You can't tell me that a **loving** God …" You have heard that statement a thousand times. Almost without exception it is the statement of someone who does not know for himself what the Word of God says. No one is qualified to impose his knowledge and his interpretation as a substitute for you having your own knowledge and your interpretation of what God says.

Imagine how many millions have lived and died without ever dreaming that God can communicate and does communicate through His Word intended for them.

Jerry Adams has dramatically shown that the answers to our questions are to be found in **knowing** the Word of God and **interpreting** it for **ourselves**.

The importance of Jerry's *CHRISTIAN BIBLE CHALLENGE* is to insist that God can communicate to you – and can do it accurately. It is up to you – individually and for yourself – to read and interpret God's Word for your life.

Ben Haden

As speaker of the CHANGED LIVES weekly worldwide TV and radio program and now through Internet Streaming of video and audio on demand, Ben Haden has been proclaiming Christ crucified and resurrected. He is now in his 45th year as a national broadcaster. He has pastored two churches -- in Miami and Chattanooga. He is a former CEO of a daily newspaper, a third-generation attorney, and an author. In the Korean War, Ben served with the CIA.

PREFACE

JESUS said, "He that believeth and is baptized [by the Holy Ghost] shall be saved." (Mark 16:16) Peter quoted Isaiah 28:16 in First Peter 2:6, "Behold, I lay in Zion a chief corner stone, elect, precious [Jesus Christ]: and he that believeth on him shall not be confounded." Hallelujah! Jesus of Nazareth is the Christ and Son of the living God.

The first and foremost duty of Christians is obedience to our commission to proclaim the gospel of Jesus Christ. Reading and studying God's Word leads to repentance which is the first prerequisite of revival. We are to love God. Love of God will prompt us to study God's Word. The more we know about God, the more obedient we will be to His commandments. And our obedience will cause us to love God even more.

Answers in this book neither alter nor substitute for anything in the Holy Bible. This book is in presentation style for easy use by Bible teachers and is intended to aid students and teachers of the Bible with relevant references to the Bible. All scriptures are quoted from the King James Version.

As a teenager I was convicted of my need of salvation when I overheard a co-worker explain to another co-worker that it was because of 'my' sins that Jesus Christ was crucified and died. Shortly thereafter, my future wife and I were baptized and later married in a Southern Baptist Church. A year or so later we were confirmed as communicants of the Episcopal Church in a parish that all my family attended. This was not a sound way to choose a church to attend, but the structure and the reverence of the Episcopal worship service appealed to us, and we gathered as a family for lunch many Sundays after church services.

The Episcopal parish we attended was involved in many Christian causes. However, Bible teaching there was less than we desired for ourselves and our children. I hungered for more understanding of God's Word and studied extensively the teachings of J. Vernon McGee, Howard C. Estep, Adrian Rogers, and other Bible expositors who broadcasted programs and published books. I was also fortunate to participate for several years in a small Bible study group led by Ted DeMoss, President of CBMC.

After fifteen years we returned to our Baptist Church home. It was wonderful. Bible teaching and preaching were powerful. How grateful to God I am for that church, its pastors, its leaders and the members. A couple of years later in 1982, I began teaching a Sunday Bible Study class and have continued to study and teach since then.

A focused Christian Bible student is the way I would describe my personal pursuit. Your succinct comments and suggestions about this book will be welcomed. Send them to me at JerryAdamsQandA@aol.com. I may not respond to you, but let me say now: Thank you and God bless you, and I will add your name to my personal prayer book with praise if your comments or suggestions prompt additions or revisions.

"May God in all things be glorified through Jesus Christ, to whom be praise and dominion for ever and ever. Amen." (I Peter 4:11)

Jerry Adams

INTRODUCTION

This book is intended to help Christians learn more about the Bible. The Bible tells Christians to "Study to shew thyself approved unto God, a workman that needeth not to be ashamed, rightly dividing the word of truth." (II Timothy 2:15)

We are told in the Bible that, "All scripture is given by inspiration of God, and is profitable for doctrine, for reproof, for correction, for instruction in righteousness: That the man of God may be perfect, thoroughly furnished unto all good works." (II Timothy 3:16/17)

In response to a question of the Sadducees, "Jesus answered and said to them, Ye do err, not knowing the scriptures, nor the power of God." (Matthew 22:29)

Paul told us that "whosoever shall call upon the name of the Lord [Jesus Christ] shall be saved." (Romans 10:13) Salvation does not require knowing and understanding scriptures, but knowing scriptures helps believers to avoid going astray and "to keep the unity of the Spirit in the bond of peace." (Ephesians 4:3)

It is hoped that the questions and answers presented will prompt you to verify the answers presented, lead you to an in-depth study of the Bible, and cause you to seek answers to other questions. Let the Holy Spirit guide you as you study the Word of God.

If you have comments about the answers presented, search the scriptures and send me your succinct answers with KJV Bible verse references at JerryAdamsQandA@aol.com. "The heart of the prudent getteth knowledge; and the ear of the wise seeketh knowledge." (Proverbs 18:15)

Non-Christians may also find the questions and answers in this book to be a source of information about Christianity. One online source of information about Christianity and the Bible is GotQuestions.org. This is a good starting point with many questions and answers presenting a variety of theological views.

At TheKingIsComing.com you can subscribe to a monthly publication of *THE BIBLE SAYS*. You can order or listen to sermons of Ben Haden at ChangedLives.org, of Joel Mullinex at RejoiceTV.org, and of Adrian Rogers at lwf.org. At TTB.org, you can listen to J. Vernon McGee's teaching of the Bible. And JAshow.org is a source of information on apologetics.

A CHRISTIAN PLEDGE OF ALLEGIANCE

I pledge allegiance to Jesus Christ
and to the righteousness of God for which He stands;
One God in three persons,
God the Father, God the Son, and God the Holy Spirit;
Looking for that blessed hope, and the glorious appearing
of the great God and our Saviour Jesus Christ;
Who gave himself for us,
that he might redeem us from all iniquity,
and purify unto himself a peculiar people,
zealous for good works.
Alleluia.

(Titus 2:13/14)

CHRISTIAN BIBLE CHALLENGE
ANSWERS EVERY CHRISTIAN SHOULD KNOW

NEW TESTAMENT QUESTIONS & ANSWERS

The Old Testament is revealed in the New Testament.

I
**How many books are there
in the King James Version of the New Testament?**
There are twenty-seven books in the New Testament.

1
What is Christianity?
Christianity is a belief and faith based on salvation by grace alone.
The Bible says, "For by grace are ye saved through faith;
and that not of yourselves: it is a gift from God:
Not of works, lest any man should boast."
(Ephesians 2:8/9)

2
What is the primary topic of the Bible?
'God's Great Love' of mankind is the primary topic of the Bible.
"God so loved the world [mankind],
that he gave his only begotten Son,
that whosoever believeth in him
should not perish, but have everlasting life."
(John 3:16)

3
What is the grand theme of the Bible?
The grand theme of the Bible is:
'The redemption of man to the glory of God.'
"For God sent not his Son into the world to condemn the world;
but that the world through him might be saved."
(John 3:17)

4
How is redemption presented in the Bible?
Redemption Planned – Genesis 1 & 2
Redemption Necessitated – Genesis 3 / 11
Redemption Provided for the Jews – Genesis 12 / Malachi
Redemption Finished and Explained by Jesus Christ – NT Gospels
Redemption Expanded to the Gentiles – Book of Acts
Redemption Expounded – NT Epistles
Redemption Fulfilled by Jesus Christ – Book of Revelation
(Colossians 1:13/14)

5
Who is the star of the Bible?
Jesus, the Christ and Son of the living God,
is the star of the Bible.
(Matthew 16:15/17)
"I Jesus have sent mine angel to testify unto you
these things in the churches.
I am the root and the offspring of David,
and the bright and morning star."
(Revelation 22:16)

6
How does Christianity differ from religions of men?
Religions of men are based in whole or in part
on man gaining God's acceptance and rewards.
No religion of men has a savior
based on faith as does Christianity.
Judaism looks for a Messiah other than Jesus Christ.

7
How does the Bible describe faith?
"Faith is the substance of things hoped for,
[and] the evidence of things not seen."
(Hebrews 11:1)

8
What are the five solas of the protestant Christianity?
Sola Fide – By Faith Alone
Sola Scriptura – By Scripture Alone
Solus Christus – By Christ Alone
Sola Gratia – By Grace Alone
Soli Deo Gloria – Glory to God Alone

9
Why does the Bible tell believers
that "faith without works is dead?"
"[Believers] are [God's] workmanship,
created in Christ Jesus unto good works,
which God hath before ordained
that we should walk in them."
(Ephesians 2:10 & James 2:20)
A believer is known by his good works
as "every tree is known by his own fruit."
(Matthew 7:16, 7:20 & 12:33 & Luke 6:44)

10
What does God's grace provide?
God's grace through faith in Jesus Christ
provides to us:
justification (Romans 3:24/26),
salvation (Titus 2:11/13),
and righteousness (Romans 5:2).

11
What is the gospel?
"The gospel [or good news] is the power of God
for everyone who believes."
(Romans 1:16)
G-O-S-P-E-L / God's Only Son Provides Everlasting Life.

12
Where in the Bible is a summary of the gospel?
The first eighteen verses of the Gospel of John
present the essence of the gospel in the person of Jesus Christ.
(John 1:1/18)

13
Where in the Bible is a believer's spiritual birth certificate?
"Verily, verily, I [Jesus] say unto you,
He that heareth [meaning accepts] my word,
and believeth on him [God the Father] that sent me,
hath everlasting life,
and shall not come into condemnation
[as nonbelievers will];
but is passed [already] from death unto life."
(John 5:24)

14
Is Christianity monotheistic?
Yes, Christianity is monotheistic.
Christian doctrine is that there is only one God,
whose name is Jehovah, the great 'I AM.'
(Exodus 3:14)
For the benefit of man,
the one and only God exists in three persons,
God the Father, God the Son, and God the Holy Spirit

15
Is the god of all religions the same god?
No, men in their religions imagine their own gods.
Evil people refuse to hear God's word [the Bible],
"but walk in the imagination of their heart,
and walk after other gods,
to serve them,
and to worship them,
shall even be their girdle,
which is good for nothing."
(Jeremiah 13:10)

16
How can there be a Trinity of God
if Christianity is monotheistic?
The Trinity describes one God as existing in three persons:
God the Father, God the Son, and God the Holy Spirit.
Jesus said,
"I and my Father are one."
(John 10:30)
The three persons of the Trinity Godhead are
equal in nature, distinct in person, and subordinate in roles.
Jesus said,
"Go ye therefore,
and teach all nations, baptizing them
in the name of the Father, and of the Son, and of the Holy Ghost."
(Matthew 28:19)

17
Will there always be a Trinity of God?
"When all things shall be subdued unto [God the Son],
then shall the Son also himself be subject unto [God the Father]
that put all things under [God the Son],
that God may be all in all."
(I Corinthians 15:28)

18
Does God love sinners?
Yes. "God commendeth his love toward us,
in that, while we were yet sinners, Christ died for us."
(Romans 5:8)

19
Who does God want to save?
"The Lord ... is longsuffering to us-ward,
not willing that any should perish,
but that all should come to repentance."
(II Peter 3:9)

20

**Where was Jesus when he said,
"A prophet is not without honor,
save in his own country, and in his own house?"**
Jesus was in Nazareth when He made this statement.
"When [Jesus] was come into his own country [Nazareth],
he taught them in their synagogue,
insomuch that they were astonished, and said,
Whence hath this man this wisdom, and these mighty works?
Is not this the carpenter's son?
is not his mother called Mary?
and his brethren, James, and Joses, and Simon, and Judas?
And his sisters, are they not all with us?
Whence then hath this man all these things?
And they were offended in him.
But Jesus said unto them,
A prophet is not without honor,
save in his own country, and in his own house."
(Matthew 13:54/57)

21

**How does the Bible say
that God views good works of a nonbeliever?**
"[Nonbelievers] are all as an unclean thing,
and all [their] righteousnesses [or works] are as filthy rags;
and we all do fade as a leaf;
and our iniquities, like the wind,
have taken us away."
(Isaiah 64:6)
This comes from Isaiah's prayer for help.

22

By what are the 'just' to live?
"The just shall live by faith."
(Habakkuk 2:4, Romans 1:17, Galatians 3:11 & Hebrews 10:38)

23
Who are the 'just'?
The 'just' are believers who have been redeemed and justified
by the shed blood of Jesus Christ.
"Without the shedding of blood is no remission."
(Hebrews 9:22)
"So shall it be at the end of the world:
the angels shall come forth, and sever the wicked from the just,
And shall cast [the wicked] into the furnace of fire:
there shall be wailing and gnashing of teeth."
(Matthew 13:49/50)

24
What should Christians do knowing what God has done for believers who have gone before us?
"Seeing we ... are [surrounded] about
with so great a cloud of witnesses,
let us lay aside every weight,
and the sin which doth so easily [ensnare] us,
and let us run with patience the race that is set before us,
Looking unto Jesus the author and finisher of our faith;
who for the joy that was set before him
endured the cross, despising the shame,
and is set down at the right hand of the throne of God."
(Hebrews 12:1/2)

25
What two things are Christians to seek first?
Christians are to seek first
the kingdom of God, and his righteousness.
"Seek ye first the kingdom of God, and his righteousness;
and all these things [life, food, drink and clothing]
shall be added unto you."
(Matthew 6:33 & Exemplified in Haggai)

26
Where in the Bible is Jesus' great invitation?
Jesus said,
"Come unto me,
all ye that labor and are heavy laden, and I will give you rest.
Take my yoke upon you, and learn of me;
for I am meek and lowly in heart:
and ye shall find rest unto your souls.
For my yoke is easy, and my burden is light."
(Matthew 11:28/30)

27
What is the blessed hope,
and where is it so stated in the Bible?
The appearing of the glory of our great God and Savior,
Jesus Christ is the blessed hope.
(Titus 2:13)
"Which hope we have as an anchor of the soul,
both sure and stedfast."
(Hebrews 6:19)

28
What is the hope that Christians have in them?
The hope [meaning assurance] that Christians have in them
is salvation --
that Jesus Christ is coming again to catch them up in the clouds,
"to meet the Lord in the air:
and so shall [they] ever be with the Lord."
(I Thessalonians 4:17 & II Peter 3:10/13)

29
Why should we trust in the Lord?
The Bible says, "It is better to trust in the Lord
than to put confidence in man."
(Psalm 118:8)

30
Who said, "I am the bread of life?"
Jesus said,
"I am the bread of life."
He also said, "This is the bread
which cometh down from heaven,
that a man may eat thereof, and not die."
(John 6:48 & 50)

31
What is man compared to the Lord?
The Lord is righteous,
"but we [before we believe] are all as an unclean thing,
and all our righteousnesses are as filthy rags;
and we all do fade as a leaf;
and our iniquities, like the wind, have taken us away."
(Isaiah 64:6)

32
Who in the Bible is called 'my son' by God?
Israel and Jesus are called my son by God.
"The Lord said unto Moses in Midian, Go, return to Egypt:
… And thou shalt say unto Pharaoh, Thus saith the Lord,
Israel is my son, even my first-born."
(Exodus 4:19 & 22)
"And Jesus, when he was baptized,
went up straightway out of the water: and, lo,
the heavens were opened unto him,
and he saw the Spirit of God
descending like a dove, and lighting upon him:
And a voice from heaven, saying,
This is my beloved Son,
in whom I am well pleased."
(Matthew 3:16/17, Mark 1:11 & Luke 3:22)
(See also Matthew 17:5 & II Peter 1:17)

33
What is the meaning of the title of 'Christ'?
'Christ' means Messiah or the anointed one.
In Christianity, Jesus is the Messiah,
who came as a Redeemer,
was rejected as the Messiah by the Jews and crucified,
is coming again as King and Lord of Israel and of all the world.
"For unto us a child is born, unto us a son is given:
and his government shall be upon his shoulder:
and his named shall be called Wonderful, Counsellor,
The mighty God, The everlasting Father, The Prince of Peace."
(Isaiah 9:6)
In Judaism, the Messiah is to be a man sent by God
to restore the kingdom of Israel.
Jews shall recognize Jesus as the Messiah when He comes again.
"and they shall look upon [him] whom they have pierced,
and they shall mourn for him, as one mourneth for his only son,
and shall be in bitterness for him,
as one in bitterness for his firstborn."
(Zechariah 12:10)

34
What is the Word?
The Word is one of the titles of Jesus Christ, God the Son.
"In the beginning was the Word,
and the Word was with God,
and the Word was God."
(John 1:1)
'Logos' is the Word of God.
'Rhema' is a Word from the Word as a Sword of the Spirit.
(Ephesians 6:17)
"[God's] Word is a lamp unto my feet, and a light unto my path."
(Psalm 119:105)

35
Did Jesus say that He is God?
The God of Christianity is a triune God –
one God existing in three persons:
God the Father, God the Son, and God the Holy Spirit.
God the Father said of Jesus,
"This is my beloved Son,
in whom I am well pleased."
(Matthew 3:17, Mark 1:11 & Luke 3:22)
Jesus said,
"I am the Son of God."
(Matthew 27:43)
Jesus said,
"I and my Father are one."
(John 10:30)
In response to the high priest's question of Jesus,
"Art thou the Christ, the Son of the Blessed,
Jesus said, I am: and ye shall see [Me]
the Son of man sitting on the right hand of power,
and coming in the clouds of heaven."
(Mark 14:61/62)
"Jesus said unto [the Jews],
Verily, verily, I say unto you,
Before Abraham was, I am."
(John 8:58)
I AM is the name of God.
"God said unto Moses, I AM THAT I AM."
(Exodus 3:14)
Jesus was crucified for saying He was God.
(Matthew 26:63/66)

36
Who said, "I am the way, the truth, and the life?"
Jesus said, "I am the way, the truth, and the life."
He also said, "No man cometh unto the Father, but by me."
(John 14:6)

37
To whom did the angel Gabriel appear?
Gabriel appeared to Daniel
(Daniel 8:16 & 9:21),
and to Joseph and to Mary
(Luke 1:19 & 1:26).

38
**What was the transfiguration,
and how does the Bible describe it?**
The transfiguration of Jesus Christ
was a manifestation of His divine glory as God the Son.
"The fashion of his countenance was altered,
and his raiment was white and glistering.
And there came a voice out of the cloud, saying,
This is my beloved Son: hear him."
(Luke 9:29 & 35 & See also Matthew 17:1/13 & Mark 9:1/8)

39
Who does the Bible say was present at the transfiguration?
Jesus was there of course; He was the one transfigured.
And Jesus' disciples, Peter, James, and John were there.
"Jesus taketh Peter, James, and John his brother,
and bringeth them up into a high mountain [mount Tabor] apart.
And [Jesus] was transfigured before them:
and [Jesus'] face did shine as the sun,
and his raiment was white as the light.
And, behold, there appeared unto [Peter, James, and John]
Moses and Elijah talking with [Jesus]."
And God the Father was there in a cloud.
"And behold a voice out of the cloud, which said,
This is my beloved Son,
in whom I am well pleased;
hear ye him."
(Matthew 17:1/3 & 5)

40
Why were Moses and Elijah present at the transfiguration?
Moses represented the law,
and Elijah represented the prophets.
The glorification of Jesus, and the instruction of God the Father
to "listen to him' made it clear that Jesus is superior
to the way of the law and the prophets.

41
What are the four gospel books of the New Testament?
Matthew, Mark, Luke and John
are the four gospel books of the New Testament.

42
Which book of the Old Testament
is considered to be a fifth gospel?
Isaiah is said to be the fifth gospel.
The Book of Isaiah presents:
(1) the virgin birth of Jesus as the Christ,
(2) the Lord's character,
(3) His life, His death, and His resurrection.
And it speaks to the coming day of the Lord.
(Isaiah 7:14 & 9:6/7)

43
Who are the two prominent Josephs in the Bible?
In the Old Testament, Joseph was a son of
Jacob (later called Israel) and Rachel.
The Book of Genesis ends with the death of Joseph in Egypt.
(Genesis 30:22/24 & 50:26)
In the New Testament, "Joseph [was] the husband of Mary,
of whom was born Jesus, who is called Christ."
(Matthew 1:16)

44
What is meant by Jesus being both God and man?
"The word was made flesh, and dwelt among us,
(and we beheld his glory,
the glory as of the only begotten of the Father,)
full of grace and truth."
(John 1:14)
The incarnation of God the Son, becoming human
yet remaining God, was a supernatural prerequisite
of Jesus dying so that "whosoever believeth in him
should not perish, but have everlasting life."
(John 3:15)

45
Who does the Bible say is guilty of sin?
The Bible says, "All have sinned,
and come short of the glory of God."
(Romans 3:23)

46
What is concupiscence?
Concupiscence is an innate tendency of man
to sin and to do evil.
God's law makes man aware of all manner of concupiscence.
(Romans 7:7/8)
Paul said, "Is the law sin? God forbid.
Nay, I had not known sin, but by the law:
for I had not known lust, except the law had said,
Thou shalt not covet.
Sin, taking occasion by the commandment,
wrought in me all manner of concupiscence.
For without the law sin was dead."
(Romans 7:7/8)
(See also Colossians 3:5 & I Thessalonians 4:5)

47
If all have sinned, how can some be saved?
"Whosoever believeth in [Jesus Christ]
shall receive remission of sins,"
(Acts 10:43)
and [is] "justified freely by [God's] grace
through the redemption that is in Christ Jesus."
(Romans 3:24)

48
What is meant by the Roman road to salvation?
The Roman Road is descriptive
of a personal witnessing guide
based on scriptures from the Book of Romans.
"For all have sinned, and come short of the glory of God;
Being justified freely by [God's] grace
through redemption that is in Christ Jesus."
(Romans 3:23/24)
"For the wages of sin is death;
but the gift of God is eternal life through Jesus Christ our Lord."
(Romans 6:23 & See also John 3:16 & Luke 13:3)
"For whosoever shall call upon the name of the Lord
shall be saved.
How then shall they call on him in whom they have not believed?
And how shall they believe in him of whom they have not heard?
And how shall they hear without a preacher?"
(Romans 10:13/14 & See also Acts 16:31)
"For with the heart man believeth unto righteousness;
and with the mouth confession is made unto salvation."
(Romans 10:9 & See also John 1:12 & Matthew 7:16 & 20)

49
Death is the consequence of what?
"The wages of sin is death."
(Romans 6:23)

50
Who can be saved?
"Through [the name of Jesus Christ]
whosoever believeth in him
shall receive remission of sins."
(Acts 10:43)
Jesus said,
"So must the Son of man be lifted up [crucified]:
That whosoever believeth in him should not perish,
but have eternal life."
(John 3:14/15)

51
How does man have knowledge of sin?
"By the law is the knowledge of sin."
(Romans 3:20)

52
Was sin in the world before the law was given?
"For until the law sin was in the world:
but sin is not imputed when there is no law.
Nevertheless, death [which is the wages of sin]
reigned from Adam to Moses,
even over them that had not sinned
after the similitude of Adam's transgression,
who is the figure of him to come."
(Romans 5:13/14)
Sin was in the world
even before the law was given.
"[And] as many as have sinned without the law
shall also perish without the law:
and as many as have sinned in the law
shall be judged by the law."
(Romans 2:12)

53

What shall fulfill the law and cover the multitude of sins?
"Above all things have fervent charity among yourselves:
for charity [love] shall cover the multitude of sins."
(I Peter 4:8)

54

What are progressive stages of rebellion against God?
The Book of Hebrews gives us five progressive stages of rebellion:
Drifting -- Not Reading the Bible or Praying
(Hebrews 2:1/4)
Doubting -- Looking More at Circumstances than at Jesus
(Hebrews 3:7 / 4:2)
Dull Hearing -- Not Accepting God's Word as Truth
(Hebrews 5:11/14)
Departing -- Not Attending Church and Willful Sinning
(Hebrews 6:1/20)
Despising -- Finding Fault and Rejecting
(Hebrews 10:26/39)
Rebellion against God generally begins with humanism;
that man is the controlling force in the world.
It progresses to self potential,
then to perceived enlightenment.
Some then become involved with sorcery,
which leads to Satanism.

55

Who said that man must be born again?
Jesus said,
"Ye must be born again."
(John 3:7)
And Jesus said,
"Verily, verily, I say unto thee,
Except a man be born again,
he cannot see the kingdom of God."
(John 3:3)

56
What does it mean to be born again?
'Born again' means to be born of the Spirit.
"That which is born of the flesh is flesh;
and that which is born of the Spirit is spirit."
(John 3:6)
"It is appointed unto [the flesh] once to die,
but after this the judgment:
So Christ was once offered to bear the sins of many;
and unto them that look for him
shall he appear the second time without sin unto salvation."
(Hebrews 9:27/28)
"And whosoever liveth [to the second coming of Jesus]
and believeth in [Jesus as the Christ and Son of the living God]
shall never die."
(John 11:26)

57
Why was Jesus born in Bethlehem
since Mary and Joseph lived in Nazareth?
"It came to pass in [the days when Mary was great with child],
that there went out a decree from Caesar Augustus,
that all the world should be taxed.
And all went to be taxed, every one into his own city.
And Joseph [and Mary] also went up [in elevation]
from Galilee, out of the city of Nazareth,
into Judea, unto the city of David,
which is called Bethlehem;
(because he was of the house and lineage of David:)
And so it was, that, while they were there,
the days were accomplished that [Mary] should be delivered.
And she brought forth her first-born son,
and wrapped him in swaddling clothes,
and laid him in a manger;
because there was no room for them in the inn."
(Luke 2:1, 3/4 & 6/7)

58
What did Jesus say when He began to preach?
"Repent: for the kingdom of heaven is at hand."
(Matthew 4:17)

59
Who were the other children of Mary, the mother of Jesus?
James, Joses, Jude, Simon and Two or More Daughters
(Matthew 27:56 & Mark 6:3)

60
Which of Mary's other sons was an apostle of Jesus?
None of Mary's other sons was an apostle.
James wrote the Book of James
and was leader of the church in Jerusalem,
but he was not an apostle.
The two apostles named James were
a son of Zebedee and a son of Alphaeus.
Jude wrote the Book of Jude,
but he was not Jude the apostle.

61
Who was Mary Magdalene?
She was a woman possessed by seven devils
who became a follower of Jesus.
(Mark 16:9 & Luke 8:2)

62
Where will the throne of the Lord's glory be?
In Jerusalem -- It is the throne of David.
"When the Son of man shall come in his glory,
and all the holy angels with him,
then shall he sit upon the throne of his glory."
(Matthew 25:31)

63
Where was Jesus baptized?
Jesus was baptized in the Jordan River near Galilee.
(Matthew 3:13)

64
What did Jesus say from the cross?
"[Jesus said], Father, forgive them;
for they know not what they do."
(Luke 23:34)
To one of the two men crucified with Jesus who said unto Jesus,
Lord, remember me when thou comest into thy kingdom,
Jesus said "Verily I say unto thee,
Today shalt thou be with me in paradise."
(Luke 23:39/43)
Jesus said, "I thirst."
(John 19:28)
"When Jesus … saw his mother,
and the disciple [John] standing by [the cross],
… he saith unto his mother, Woman, behold thy son!
Then saith he to [John], Behold thy mother!"
(John 19:26)
"Jesus cried with a loud voice, saying, Eli, Eli, lama sabachthani?
that is to say, My God, my God, why hast thou forsaken me?"
(Matthew 27:46)
"And when Jesus had cried with a loud voice,
he said, It is finished. [and]
Father, into thy hands I commend my spirit:
and having said thus, he gave up the ghost."
(Luke 23:46 & John 19:30)

65
Why did Jesus tell believers to be of good cheer?
Jesus said,
"Be of good cheer for I have overcome the world."
(John 16:33)

66
How can man overcome the world?
Man can overcome the world through faith that Jesus is the Christ.
"Who is he that overcometh the world,
but he that believeth that Jesus is the Son of God."
(I John 5:5)

67
What shall man obtain in overcoming the world?
"To him that overcometh will I [Jesus Christ]
give to eat of the tree of life,
which is in the midst of the paradise of God."
(Revelation 2:7)
"He that overcometh shall not be hurt of the second death."
(Revelation 2:11)
"He that overcometh, the same shall be clothed in white raiment;
and I [Jesus Christ] will not blot out his name
out of the book of life,
but I will confess his name before my Father, and before angels."
(Revelation 3:5)
"He that overcometh shall inherit all things;
and I [God the Father] will be his God, and he shall be my son."
(Revelation 21:7)

68
Which Book of the Bible is oftentimes referred to as the Constitution of Christianity?
The Book of Romans is said to be
the Constitution of Christianity.
It is thought to be the most complete summary
of Christian doctrine.
The Book of Romans is also referred to as
The Christian Manifesto,
and The Cathedral of the Christian Faith.

69
What is a parable?
A parable is an illustration of a Bible truth.

70
Why did Jesus begin to speak in parables?
Jesus said,
"I speak to them [nonbelievers] in parables:
because they seeing see not;
and hearing they hear not,
neither do they understand."
(Matthew 13:13)
"[And] because it is given unto you [believers]
to know the mysteries of the kingdom of heaven,
but to them it is not given
[because they do not believe]."
(Matthew 13:11)

71
Which chapter of the Bible
presents the most parables of Jesus?
Chapter 13 of the Book of Matthew
is the Mystery Parable Discourse of Jesus.
It presents seven parables,
which is more than in any other chapter of the Bible:
the parable of the sower,
the parable of the wheat and the tares,
the parable of the mustard seed,
the parable of the leaven,
the parable of the hidden treasure,
the parable of the pearl of great value,
and the parable of the net.
(Matthew 13:1/52)

72

**In the parables of Jesus, who is represented by
the hidden treasure and the pearl of great price?**
Man is the hidden treasure and the pearl of great price.
(Matthew 13:44/46)

73

**Who is represented by the man
who found the treasure in the field
and the merchant who found the pearl of great price?**
The finder of the treasure and the pearl of great price is Jesus.
(Matthew 13:44/46)

74

**In Jesus' parable of the lost son,
which was the prodigal son - the older or the younger son?**
It was the younger son who was the prodigal son.
(Luke 15:12/13)

75

What does the parable of the lost son picture?
It pictures God the Father's divine love, and mercy, and grace.
The prodigal son was lost but he came to repentance,
and his father graciously restored him to the family
just as God will restore lost sinners who repent.
(Luke 15:22/24)

76

**In the parable of the good Samaritan,
where was the man who fell among thieves left for dead?**
"A certain man went down from Jerusalem to Jericho,
and fell among thieves, which stripped him of his raiment,
and wounded him, and departed, leaving him half dead."
(Luke 10:30)

77
Why is the Samaritan called the good Samaritan?
When a priest and a Levite saw the wounded man
who fell among thieves,
they passed by him on the other side of the road.
But the Samaritan, when he saw the man,
had compassion on him
and cared for him as a neighbor.
(Luke 10:31/36)

78
**What is the 'golden rule'
and where is it stated in the Bible?**
"All things whatsoever ye would
that men should do to you,
do ye even so to them."
It is from Jesus' sermon on the mount at Matthew 7:12.
It is often quoted as
'Do unto others as you would have them do unto you.'

79
**Where else in the Bible did Jesus use the phrase
"all things whatsoever"?**
Matthew 21:22,
"All things, whatsoever ye shall ask in prayer,
believing,
ye shall receive."
(Matthew 28:20), and
"Go ye therefore, and teach all nations,
baptizing them in the name of the Father,
and of the Son, and of the Holy Ghost:
Teaching them to observe all things
whatsoever I have commanded you."
(Matthew 28:19/20)

80
What timing does the Bible give for predestination?
Predestination does not mean that God chose
before the foundation of the world
who would be saved and who would not be saved,
as some mistakenly teach.
But God did predestinate to eternal life with Him
"[whosoever believeth] in him
before the foundation of the world,
that [believers] should be holy and without blame
before him in love: Having predestinated [believers] unto
the adoption of children by Jesus Christ to himself,
according to the good pleasure of his will,
To the praise of the glory of his grace,
wherein he hath made [believers] accepted
in the beloved [Jesus Christ].
In whom we have redemption through his blood,
the forgiveness of sins,
according to the riches of his grace."
(Ephesians 1:4/7)

81
What things defile a man?
"Things which proceed out of the mouth
come forth from the heart; and they defile the man.
For out of the heart proceed evil thoughts,
murders, adulteries, fornications,
thefts, false witness, [and] blasphemies:
These are the things which defile a man."
(Matthew 15:1/20)

82
What is the New Testament guide to giving?
"As he purposes in his heart so let him give;
for God loves a cheerful giver."
(II Corinthians 9:7)

83
Who were the apostles of Jesus Christ?

Peter* - The Apostle of Hope (His former name was Simon)

James** - (Son of Zebedee)

John** - The Apostle of Love (Brother of James)

Andrew* (Brother of Peter)

Philip

Bartholomew (Nathanael)

Matthew

Thomas

James (Son of Alphaeus)

Jude - (A brother of James*** - Luke 6:16)

(Also Judas, Thaddeaus & Lebbaeus - Matthew 10:3)

(Also Judas, not Judas Iscariot - John 14:22)

Simon the Zealot

Judas Iscariot - (The traitor - Luke 6:16)

* Peter and Andrew were brothers.

** Boanerges (The sons of thunder - Mark 3:17)

*** Probably James the son of Alphaeus

(Matthew 10:1/4, Mark 3:16/19, Luke 6:13/16, and Acts 1:13)

Who replaced Judas Iscariot as an apostle?

(Matthias - Acts1:26)

So, who was Paul?

Paul was the apostle to the Gentiles.

Paul was the apostle of faith.

Paul was Saul of the tribe of Benjamin.

(John) Mark, Luke and Timothy were disciples
who ministered with Paul.

84
How do men call upon the name of the Lord?
"If thou shalt confess with thy mouth the Lord Jesus
[that Jesus is the Son of the living God
and the Christ who died for your sins],
and shalt believe in thine heart that God [the Father]
hath raised [Jesus] from the dead,
thou shalt be saved.
For with the heart
man believeth unto righteousness;
and with the mouth
confession is made unto salvation."
(Romans 10:9/10)

85
Who was present at the transfiguration of Jesus Christ?
Jesus Christ was there of course.
Peter, James and John were there.
Moses and Elijah were there.
And God the Father was there in a bright cloud.
(Matthew 17:1/13)

86
Who did Jesus say would be greatest in heaven?
"Jesus called a little child unto him,
and set him in the midst of the disciples.
And [Jesus] said, Verily, I say unto you,
except ye be converted,
and become as little children,
ye shall not enter into the kingdom of heaven.
Whosoever therefore shall humble himself
as this little child,
the same is greatest in the kingdom of heaven."
(Matthew 18:1/5)

87
How many people does the Lord want to save?
"The Lord … is longsuffering to us-ward,
not willing that any should perish,
but that all should come to repentance."
(II Peter 3:9)

88
Did Jesus say that a rich man
cannot enter into the kingdom of heaven?
Jesus, in responding to a rich young ruler
who declared that he had kept six commandments
Jesus enumerated to him, said,
"If thou wilt be perfect,
Go and sell that thou hast, and give to the poor,
and thou shalt have treasure in heaven:
and come and follow me."
(Matthew 19:21)
When the rich young ruler went away,
Jesus said,
"Verily I say unto you, That a rich man
shall hardly enter into the kingdom of heaven.
[For] it is easier for a camel to go through the eye of a needle,
than for a rich man to enter into the kingdom of God."
(Matthew 19:16/26)
Worldly riches make it harder for some to follow Christ;
however, the issue presented here is that
the rich young ruler was trying to get to heaven on his own.
Eternal life cannot be attained of yourself.
Eternal life is a gift from God to whosoever believeth
in Jesus as the Christ and the Son of God.
(John 3:14/16 & Ephesians 2:8)
This is also true for the poor,
but in the days of Jesus here on earth,
it was thought that the rich were blessed of God.

89
What were Jesus' four major Bible discourses?
Jesus' four major Bible discourses were:
the Sermon on the Mount (Matthew 5, 6 & 7),
the Mystery Parable Discourse (Matthew 13),
the Olivet Discourse (Matthew 24 & 25),
and the Upper Room Discourse (John 13, 14, 15, 16 & 17).

90
How can you be assured of your salvation?
Being baptized by the Holy Ghost and
having the Spirit of God within you
is your assurance
that Jesus has redeemed you unto salvation.
Can you say that Jesus is the Lord and really mean it?
This is how we know that we know.
"The Spirit itself beareth witness with our spirit,
that we are the children of God."
(Romans 8:16)

91
Who was the father of Joseph,
the husband of Mary, of whom was born Jesus?
Two different names of Joseph's father are given in the Bible.
"Jacob begat Joseph the husband of Mary,
of whom was born Jesus, who is the Christ."
(Matthew 1:16)
"Jesus himself began to be about thirty years of age,
being (as was supposed) the son of Joseph,
which was the son of Heli [Eli]."
(Luke 3:23)
It is thought by many that Jacob was Joseph's father,
and Heli [Eli] was Joseph's father-in-law
and the father of Mary.

92
What was the day of Pentecost?
When Jesus,
after His resurrection and before His ascension,
was "assembled together with [His eleven apostles],
[He] commanded them that they should not depart from Jerusalem,
but wait for the promise of the Father"
to send the Comforter, which is the Holy Ghost [Spirit].
(Mark 16:14, Acts 1:4 & John 14:16 & 26)
"And when the day of Pentecost was fully come,
they were all with one accord in one place.
And suddenly there came a sound from heaven
as of a rushing mighty wind,
and it filled all the house where they were sitting.
And there appeared unto them cloven tongues like as of fire,
and it sat upon each of them.
And they were all filled with the Holy Ghost."
(Acts 2:1/4)
And Peter preached the gospel of Jesus Christ
unto the men of Judea and of Jerusalem,
and told them that the coming of the Holy Spirit
was the fulfillment of the prophecy of Joel.
(Acts 2:14/40)

93
What was the primary theme of Peter's sermon on the day of Pentecost?
The resurrection of the Lord Jesus Christ.
This is also the theme of the Book of Acts.

94
What was unique about Peter's message on the day of Pentecost?
"Every man heard [Peter's message] in his own language."
(Acts 2:1/8)

95
What is the 'law of sin'?
The 'law of sin' is the evil nature of man's flesh.
Paul referenced the 'law of sin' in the Book of Romans,
and in the Book of Galatians, Paul said,
"The flesh lusteth against the Spirit,
and the Spirit against the flesh:
and these are contrary the one to the other:
so that ye cannot do the things that ye would."
(Romans 7:23, 7:25 & 8:2 & Galatians 5:17)
"The works of the flesh are manifest, which are these;
adultery, fornication, uncleanness, lasciviousness,
idolatry, witchcraft, hatred, [contentiousness], [jealousies],
wrath, [selfish ambitions], [dissensions], heresies,
envying, murders, drunkenness, revellings, and such like."
(Galatians 5:19/21)

96
How can man avoid the 'law of sin'?
"[By being] led of the Spirit,
ye are not under the law [of sin]."
(Galatians 5:18)

97
What is sin, and who has sinned?
Sin is a violation of a religious or moral law.
"Sin is the transgression of [God's] law."
(I John 3:4)
Sin is also deliberate disobedience
to a known will of God.
"To him that knoweth to do good, and doeth it not,
to him it is sin."
(James 4:17)
"All have sinned, and come short of the glory of God."
(Romans 3:23)

98

What does the Bible say about Adam's sin?

By Adam's violation
of God's command in the garden of Eden,
"sin entered into the world, and death by sin;
and so death passed upon all men,
for that all have sinned."
(Romans 5:12)
Adam's sin is referred to as 'original sin'
which is ascribed, reckoned or imputed to all men.
Even though the Bible says that
"sin is not imputed when there is no law,
sin was in the world [before the law]."
[And] death reigned from Adam to Moses
[before the law was given],
even over them that had not sinned
after the [like manner] of Adam's transgression."
(Romans 5:13/14)

99

What is an English word for the Greek word apostle?

An English word for apostle is messenger.
Jesus told His apostles to "Go … and teach all nations,
baptizing them in the name of the Father,
and of the Son, and of the Holy Ghost:
Teaching them to observe all things whatsoever
I [Jesus] commanded you,
even unto the end of the world."
(Matthew 28:19/20)

100

Who was the apostle to the Gentiles?

Paul said, "I speak to you Gentiles,
inasmuch as I am the apostle of the Gentiles."
(Romans 11:13)

101
**What does the Bible mean that,
'as by one man death reigned, so by one man life reigns'?**
Adam was "the figure of him [Jesus Christ] that was to come."
(Romans 5:14)
"But [the free gift of him that was to come
is not like the offense of Adam].
For if through the offense of one [Adam] many be dead,
much more the grace of God, and the gift by grace,
which is by one man, Jesus Christ, hath abounded unto many.
[The gift is not like that
which came through the one man, Adam, who sinned],
but the free gift is of many offenses unto justification.
For if by one man's offense death reigned by one;
much more they which receive abundance of grace
and of the gift of righteousness
shall reign in life by one [man], Jesus Christ."
(Romans 5:15/17)
Many people think it unfair that Adam's sin is imputed to all men,
but no one complains that his penalty of death
was paid by one man,
Jesus Christ, for all men who believe in Him.

102
How many of Paul's epistles are Books of the Bible?
Thirteen of Paul's epistles are Books of the Bible.
Romans, I & II Corinthians, Galatians, Ephesians,
Philippians, Colossians, I & II Thessalonians,
I & II Timothy, Titus, and Philemon.
The Book of Hebrews may also be an epistle of Paul's.

103
Who sought out Paul in Rome and found him?
Onesiphours
(II Timothy 1:17)

104
Which of Paul's epistles did he write from prison in Rome?
The Bible tells us that
Ephesians, Philippians, Colossians and Philemon
were written by the apostle Paul
while he was incarcerated in Rome.
(Acts 28:16 & 30/31)
Paul was also imprisoned in Caesarea,
but there he was not allowed to have visitors or to share the gospel
as he was in Rome, where he was in home confinement.

105
Is death a certainty for all men and women?
Yes, death is a certainty
with the only exception being the believers
who are alive and remain
at the time of the rapture of believers.
"The Lord God commanded the man, saying,
Of every tree of the garden thou mayest freely eat:
But of the tree of the knowledge of good and evil,
thou shalt not eat of it:
for in the day that thou eatest thereof thou shalt surely die."
(Genesis 2:16/17)
"It is appointed unto men once to die, but after this the judgment."
(Hebrews 9:27)
Enoch and Elijah were taken to heaven without dying.
Some think that these two men will come back to earth
as God's two witnesses, be killed,
and resurrected after three and a half days.
(Revelation 11:1/14)

106
**What was the name of the high priest's servant
whose ear was smote off by Peter?**
The servant's name was Malchus.
(John 18:10)

107
What was the last miracle of Jesus before His crucifixion?
Jesus' last miracle before His crucifixion
was to heal the ear of the high priest's servant
after Peter smote it off with his sword.
(Luke 22:51)

108
**How many people will be saved
and how many people will be lost?**
Few people will be saved
compared to many people who will be lost.
Jesus said,
"Enter ye in at the strait gate:
for wide is the gate, and broad is the way,
that leadeth to destruction,
and many there be which go in thereat:
Because strait is the gate, and narrow is the way,
which leadeth unto life, and few there be that find it."
(Matthew 7:13/14)

109
Why did God give man the law?
God gave man the law
so that man would have knowledge of sin.
Paul said,
"Now we know that what things soever the law saith,
it saith to them who are under the law:
that every mouth may be stopped
[from making excuses of not having knowledge of sin],
and all the world may become guilty before God.
Therefore by the deeds of the law
there shall no flesh be justified in [God's] sight:
for by the law is the knowledge of sin."
(Romans 3:19/20)

110
What are the major themes of the Book of Acts?
The major themes of the Book of Acts are
the indwelling of the Holy Spirit,
and the works of Peter and Paul
in carrying out the Great Commission
to build the church.
(Acts 1:4, 2:1/4 & 9:1/28:31)

111
Was Stephen one of Jesus' apostles?
Stephen was not one of the twelve apostles,
but "Stephen [was] full of faith and power,
[and] did great wonders and miracles among the people."
He was one of seven men chosen of Jesus' disciples
to minister to the needs of the people.
(Acts 6:1 & 8)
Stephen was falsely accused and was stoned to death
for his defense of Jesus Christ
which is recorded in Acts, chapter 7.
(Acts 6:11/13)

112
Who is forbidden to be a prophet?
"And Moses said unto [Joshua], Enviest thou for my sake?
would God that all the Lord's people were prophets,
and that the Lord would put his spirit upon them!"
(Numbers 11:28/29)

113
**What will the Lord God do
without revealing it to His prophets?**
"Surely the Lord God will do nothing,
but he revealeth his secret unto his servants the prophets."
(Amos 3:7)

114
What is the subject of Bible prophecy?
Israel, the people and the nation;
Palestine, the land;
Jerusalem, the city;
and Jesus Christ, the Messiah,
King and the Son of the Living God.
The church is the subject of revelation
and not the subject of prophecy.

115
What is the theme of Bible prophecy?
The theme of Bible prophecy is
the second coming of Jesus Christ to make all things right.
(I Corinthians 15:25)

116
What is the spirit of prophecy?
"The testimony of Jesus is the spirit of prophecy."
(Revelation 19:10)

117
What is the evidence
that there is coming a day of judgment?
The evidence that a judgment day is coming
is that Jesus died and was raised from the dead.
"[God the Father] has commanded all men everywhere
to repent:
Because he has appointed a day,
in which he will judge the world
in righteousness by that man [Jesus]
whom he has ordained;
whereof he has given assurance unto all men,
in that he has raised [Jesus] from the dead."
(Acts 17:30/31)

118
What will be the next world power?
The ten nations of the revived Roman empire
under rule of the Antichrist.
(Daniel 2:33/25)

119
**For what period of time
does the Antichrist reign on earth?**
Forty-Two Months -- Known as the Great Tribulation
"There was given unto [the beast]
a mouth speaking great things and blasphemies;
and power was given unto him to continue
forty and two months."
(Revelation 13:5)

120
**For what period of time do the two witnesses of God
prophesy on earth?**
The two witnesses of God prophesy 1260 days
during the last half of the Tribulation Period.
"I [the Lord] will give power unto my two witnesses,
and they shall prophesy
a thousand two hundred and three score days,
clothed in sackcloth."
(Revelation 11:3)

121
What do the two end time witnesses prophesy?
The two witnesses of God prophesy of repentance
and of the coming day of the Lord.
Sackcloth is indicative of repentance.
And the third woe shall come quickly after the second woe.
(Revelation 11)

122

**Beside the two witnesses who else will be preaching
to the people on the earth during the end times?**
The Bible says that an angel
will be preaching to the people on earth.
"And I saw another angel fly in the midst of heaven,
having the everlasting gospel to preach
unto them that dwell on the earth,
and to every nation, and kindred, and tongue, and people,
saying with a loud voice, Fear God, and give glory to him;
for the hour of his judgment is come:
and worship him that made heaven, and earth,
and the sea, and the fountains of waters."
(Revelation 14:6/7)

123

What will happen to the two end time witnesses of God?
"When they shall have finished their testimony,
the beast that ascendeth out of the bottomless pit
shall make war against them, and shall overcome them,
and kill them.
And their dead bodies shall lie in the street [of Jerusalem]
… [for] three days and a half …
[then] the spirit of life from God [shall] enter into them,
and they [shall stand] upon their feet …
and ascend up to heaven."
(Revelation 11:7/11)

124

**What is the hidden truth of John's vision
in chapter one of the Book of Revelation?**
A preview of the church in all the ages.
"The seven stars are the angels of the seven churches:
and the seven candlesticks … are the seven churches."
(Revelation 1:20)

125
Is the Book of Revelation a book of prophecy?
Yes. See Revelation 22:18.
But it is primarily a book of revelation.

126
What happens to the church in Revelation 4:1?
The church is caught up into heaven with believers of all ages.
"I [John] looked, and, behold, a door was opened in heaven:
and the first voice which I heard
was as it were of a trumpet talking with me;
which said, Come up hither."
(Revelation 4:1)
This event is the resurrection and rapture of believers.

127
**What is the difference between
the resurrection and the rapture of believers?**
The bodies of the saved of all ages, being the dead in Christ,
shall be raised or resurrected first and reunited with their souls.
(I Thessalonians 4:16/17)
Then believers living at the time "shall be caught up
[raptured] together with [the resurrected dead in Christ]
in the clouds, to meet the Lord in the air:
and so shall we ever be with the Lord."
(I Thessalonians 4:17)
"We shall not all sleep [or die], but we shall all be changed,
In a moment, in the twinkling of an eye,
at the last trump: for the trumpet shall sound,
and the dead shall be raised incorruptible,
and we [which are alive and remain] shall be changed.
(I Corinthians 15:51/52)

128
What is the theme of the Books of Thessalonians?
Jesus Christ's second coming as King of Israel
and as King of kings and Lord of lords of the world.

129
What group is mentioned 111 times in the New Testament, but only once after chapter three of the Book of Revelation?
The Church is not mentioned in the Bible
after chapter three of the Book of Revelation.
(Revelation 3:22 & 22:16)

130
**Where were the seven churches
of the Book Revelation located?**
The seven churches were in Asia at Ephesus, Smyrna,
Pergamos, Thyatira, Sardis, Philadelphia and Laodicea.
(Revelation 1:11)
Each church represents
a state of the church in progressive ages.

131
**What is opened in the Book of Revelation,
chapter 19, verse 11?**
Heaven is opened.
Heaven must be closed at that time for it to be opened.

132
**What in the Bible supports that believers
are resurrected and raptured in Revelation 4:1?**
When chapter three of the Book of Revelation closes
the scene is of the churches on earth.
In chapters four and five of the Book of Revelation
the scene shifts to heaven and believers of all ages
are there worshiping God.
(Revelation 4 & 5)

133
How are the resurrection and rapture of believers described in the Bible?
"The Lord himself shall descend from heaven
with a shout,
with the voice of the archangel,
and with the trump of God:
and the dead in Christ shall rise first:
Then we [believers] which are alive and remain
shall be caught up [raptured] together with them in the clouds,
to meet the Lord in the air:
and so shall we ever be with the Lord."
(I Thessalonians 4:16/17)
This takes place in Revelation 4:1.

134
What shall be swallowed up in victory?
Death is swallowed up in victory after the millennial kingdom.
(Isaiah 25:8 & I Corinthians 15:54)

135
What are the sting of death and the strength of sin?
"The sting of death is sin;
and the strength of sin is the law.
But thanks be to God,
which giveth us the victory through our Lord Jesus Christ."
(I Corinthians 15:56/57)
"O death, where is thy sting? O grave, where is thy victory?"
(I Corinthians 15:55)

136
What is the closing benediction of the Bible?
"The grace of our Lord Jesus Christ be with you all. Amen."

137
What are the two end-time suppers prophesied in the Bible?
The marriage supper of the Lamb
will be for all believers who are raptured to heaven.
"Blessed are they which are called
unto the marriage supper of the Lamb.
(Revelation 19:9)
The supper of the great God
will be here on earth after the battle at Armageddon.
The fowl will eat the flesh of those killed in the battle.
"And I [John] saw an angel standing in the sun;
and he cried with a loud voice, saying
to all the fowls that fly in the midst of heaven,
Come and gather yourselves together
unto the supper of the great God;
That ye may eat the flesh of kings,
and the flesh of captains, and the flesh of mighty men,
and the flesh of horses, and of them that sit on them,
and the flesh of all men, both free and bond, both small and great."
(Revelation 19:17/18)

138
What is the judgment seat of Christ?
"[Believers] must all appear before the judgment seat of Christ;
that every one may receive the things done in his body,
according to that he hath done, whether it be good or bad."
(II Corinthians 5:10)
The judgment seat of Christ will take place
after the rapture of believers.
Nonbelievers will be judged at the great white throne
for their sins and their failure to accept Jesus as the Christ.
(Revelation 20:11)
The judgment of nonbelievers happens
after the Millennial kingdom of Jesus Christ here on earth.

139
What works of a believer will be judged?
Only works of a believer
after he or she repents and calls on the Lord
shall be judged at the Judgment Seat of Christ.
Works before we are born again are not unto the Lord.
And when we call on the Lord and confess our sins,
our sins are forgiven.
"As far as the east is from the west, so far hath [the Lord]
removed our transgressions from us."
(Psalm 103:12)

140
What was the key to the first coming of Jesus Christ?
The virgin birth was the key
to the first coming of Jesus Christ.
"The Lord himself shall give you a sign;
Behold, a virgin shall conceive, and bear a son,
and shall call his name Immanuel."
(Isaiah 7:14)

141
What is the key to the second coming of Jesus Christ?
What is happening in Jerusalem and to the Jews
is the key to the second coming of Jesus Christ.
Jesus' disciples came to Him asking:
"What shall be the sign of thy coming,
and the end of the world?
And Jesus answered,"
telling them what would happen
before His second coming
and saying:
"When ye shall see all these things,
know that it is near, even at the doors."
(Matthew 24)

142

**Who was John the Baptist,
and why was he called 'the Baptist'?**
John the Baptist was the forerunner of Jesus Christ.
John the Baptist "is
he that was spoken of by the prophet Isaiah,
saying, The voice of one crying in the wilderness,
Prepare ye the way of the Lord,
make his paths straight."
(Isaiah 40:3, Matthew 3:3, Mark 1:3, Luke 3:4 & John 1:23)
Jesus said of John the Baptist,
"Verily I say unto you,
Among them that are born of women
there hath not risen a greater than John the Baptist."
(Matthew 11:11)
John the Baptist's message was, "Repent ye:
for the kingdom of heaven is at hand."
And he baptized all who confessed their sins.
(Matthew 3:2 & 5/6)

143

What does the Bible say was the role of John the Baptist?
"There was a man sent from God,
whose name was John [the Baptist]."
(John 1:6)
"[John the Baptist] came for a witness,
to bear witness of the Light,
that all men [not just the Jews] through [Jesus] might believe."
(John 1:7)
"[John the Baptist] was not that Light,
but was sent to bear witness of that Light."
(John 1:8)

144
How did mankind respond to Jesus at His first coming?
"[Jesus] was in the world,
and the world was made by him,
and the world knew him not."
(John 1:10)
"[Jesus] came unto his own [meaning the children of Israel],
and his own [people the Jews] received him not."
(John 1:11)
Some, however, [including Jews and Gentiles] did receive Him.
and "as many as received him
[by believing Jesus to be the Christ],
to them [Jesus] gave power to become the sons of God,
even to them that believe on [Jesus'] name."
(John 1:12)

145
Is the 'Word of God' the message or the messenger?
When 'Word' is capitalized,
it is used as a title of Jesus Christ.
"In the beginning was the Word,
and the Word was with God, and the Word was God."
(John 1:1)
"His name is called The Word of God."
(Revelation 19:13)
The 'word of God' is descriptive of God's message.
"They [the assembled believers]
were filled with the Holy Ghost,
and they spake the word of God with boldness."
(Acts 4:31)
At Antioch, "came almost the whole city together
to hear the word of God."
(Acts 13:44)
The 'word of God' is the sword of the Spirit.
(Ephesians 6:17)

146
What is 'the Sermon on the Mount'?
What is known as 'the Sermon on the Mount'
was one of Jesus' four major discourses recorded in the Bible.
It appears in Matthew, chapters five, six and seven.
In this sermon, Jesus taught the spiritual character and qualities
of the kingdom of God to the disciples who sought Him.
Few of the multitudes had followed Jesus up into the mountain.
The sermon presents the Beatitudes,
it describes Christians as the salt of the earth
and the light of the world,
and it tells us that Christ came to fulfill the law.
In the sermon, Jesus taught us about anger, about adultery,
about divorce, and about oaths.
Jesus told us to love our enemies,
and to give our alms in private.
He taught us how to pray and about fasting.
He told us to store our treasures in heaven,
and explained that the light of the body is the eye.
Jesus said that we are to trust one master,
not to judge or condemn others.
He gave us the golden rule, and told us that
we can enter the kingdom of heaven
only through the strait gate.
He warned us about false prophets
and told us what will happen to them.
He compared Himself to the foundation of rock
and all other foundations to sand.
And Jesus detailed the Gospel of the Kingdom.

147
What is the first and great commandment?
"Thou shalt love the Lord thy God with all thy heart,
and with all thy soul, and with all thy mind."
(Matthew 22:37/38)

148
What are the Beatitudes?
The Beatitudes are blessings Jesus declared
at the beginning of His Sermon on the Mount.
(Matthew 5:1/12)
"Blessed be the Lord, who daily loadeth us with benefits,
even the God of our salvation."
(Psalm 68:19)

149
What is the meaning of 'sleeping' in the Bible?
'Sleeping' in the Bible refers to the state of the body
of a believer who has died.
The Bible does not speak of the soul sleeping.
Paul wrote that the soul of a believer
being absent from the body
is present with the Lord.
(I Corinthians 5:3 & 8)

150
What is the commandment like unto first?
"And the second is like unto [the first],
Thou shalt love thy neighbor as thyself."
(Matthew 22:39)

151
On what two commandments
do all the law and the prophets hang?
The first and second of the ten commandments.
"Thou shalt love the Lord thy God with all thy heart,
and with all thy soul, and with all thy mind.
And the second is like unto [the first],
Thou shalt love thy neighbor as thyself.
On these two commandments hang all the law and the prophets."
(Matthew 22:37/40)

152
Who is referred to in the Bible as the 'other Mary'?
The 'other Mary' appears in the Bible at the sepulcher
where Jesus was laid by Joseph of Arimathaea.
(Matthew 27:61 & 28:1)
She is probably Mary the mother of James the less
and the wife of Alphaeus [Greek for Cleophas].
(Matthew 27:56 & Mark 15:40)
Mary the mother of Jesus,
and Mary the wife of Cleophas
were sisters.
(John 19:25)

153
What is meant by "the Word was made flesh"?
'The Word' or 'Logos' is a title of Deity.
Flesh describes humanity.
Incarnation is the miracle of God the Son
becoming humanity.
"In the beginning was the Word,
and the Word was with God,
and the Word was God."
(John 1:1)
"And the Word was made flesh, and dwelt among us,
(and we beheld his glory,
the glory as of the only begotten of the Father,)
full of grace and truth."
(John 1:14)

154
How can a Christian avoid the lust of the flesh?
"Walk in the Spirit, and ye shall not fulfil
the lust of the flesh."
(Galatians 5:16)

155
Who was the apostle, Andrew's father?
Jona (also Jonah & Jonas) was the father of Simon,
who was Andrew's brother.
(Matthew 4:18, Mark 1:16, Luke 6:14 & John 1:40, 6:8 & 21:15/17)

156
Who of the twelve apostles was first to follow Jesus?
Andrew was the first of the twelve apostles to follow Jesus.
(John 1:35/40)

157
What is the difference between 'the time of the end' and 'the end of time'?
'The time of the end' refers to the end of the Church Age
leading to the rapture of believers,
the Tribulation period,
and the second coming of Jesus Christ to the earth.
'The end of time' is when Jesus Christ
delivers up the kingdom to God the Father,
the heavens and earth are burned up,
and all unbelievers appear
before the White Throne Judgment.

158
Who are the 'dragon,' the 'beast,' and the 'false prophet' in the Book of Revelation?
The dragon is Satan,
the beast is the Antichrist,
and the false prophet is a renowned religious leader.
(Revelation 20:2, 13:2/4, 13:11/14, 16:13, 19:20 & 20:10)
'Beast' is used in chapters 4, 5 and 6, and in 14:3, 15:7 and 19:4
to mean living being and not the Antichrist.

159
Who of the twelve apostles did Jesus see under the fig tree?
Jesus saw Nathanael under the fig tree.
(John 1:45/50)

160
**When did the regathering
of the children of Israel to her land begin?**
The children of Israel began returning to their land
on December 9, 1917
after General Allenby secured Jerusalem from the Turks.
From the Babylonian captivity which began in 605 B.C.
through May 14, 1948 (2,518 years),
Israel did not exist as a nation.
Effective May 15, 1948, Israel became a nation again,
fulfilling the Word of God, as prophesied by the prophet Isaiah
six hundred years before the first coming of Jesus Christ.
"Who hath heard such a thing? who hath seen such things?
Shall the earth be made to bring forth in one day?
or shall a nation be born at once?
for as soon as Zion travailed, she brought forth her children."
(Isaiah 66:8)

161
Is Jehovah a God of love?
Yes, Jehovah is a God of love.
"God so loved the world [mankind],
that he gave his only begotten Son,
that whosoever believeth in him
should not perish, but have everlasting life."
(John 3:16)
But Jehovah is also a God of wrath.
The Bible tells us that the day of God's wrath is coming
upon those "who believed not the truth,
but had pleasure in unrighteousness."
(II Thessalonians 2:12)

162
What is the writer's purpose in the Book of Hebrews?
To encourage believers
to keep their faith in Jesus as the Christ.
"For we are made partakers of Christ,
if we hold the beginning of our confidence
steadfast unto the end [or until our bodily death]."
(Hebrews 3:14)

163
To whom is the Book of Hebrews addressed?
The Book of Hebrews was addressed to:
"Holy brethren [both Jews and Gentiles],
partakers of the heavenly calling."
(Hebrews 3:1)

164
**How do Christians know
that they will not go through the Tribulation period?**
"The Lord will take vengeance on his adversaries,
and he reserveth wrath for his enemies."
(Nahum 1:2)
"God hath not appointed us [believers] to wrath,
but to obtain salvation by our Lord Jesus Christ,
who died for us, that, whether we wake or sleep,
we should live together with him."
(I Thessalonians 5:9/10)

165
Why does the Bible tell wives
to submit unto their own husbands?

The Bible makes marriage symbolic of the church.
"Wives, submit yourselves unto your own husbands,
as unto the Lord.
For the husband is the head of the wife,
even as Christ is the head of the church:
and he is the savior of the body.
Therefore as the church is subject unto Christ,
so let the wives be to their own husbands in every thing."
(Ephesians 5:22/24)
The greater responsibility is charged to husbands.
"Husbands, love your wives,
even as Christ also loved the church,
and gave himself for it;
That he might sanctify and cleanse it
with the washing of water by the word.
That he might present it to himself
a glorious church,
not having spot, or wrinkle, or any such thing;
but that it should be holy and without blemish.
So ought men to love their wives as their own bodies.
He that loveth his wife loveth himself.
For no man ever yet hated his own flesh;
but nourisheth and cherisheth it,
even as the Lord the church:
For we are all members of [Christ's] body,
of his flesh, and of his bones.
For this cause shall a man leave his father and mother,
and shall be joined unto his wife, and the two shall be one flesh.
This is a great mystery:
but I [Paul] speak concerning Christ and the church.
Nevertheless let every one of you [husbands] in particular
so love his wife even as himself;
and the wife see that she reverence her husband."
(Ephesians 5:25/33)

166
**Who were the three women
who went to the sepulcher where Jesus was buried
early in the morning on the first day after the sabbath?**
"And when the Sabbath was past,
Mary Magdalene, and Mary the mother of James, and Salome,
had brought sweet spices
that they might come and anoint [Jesus].
And very early in the morning
the first day of the week [Sunday],
they came unto the sepulcher at the rising of the sun."
(Mark 16:1/2)

167
**What did the three women find
on the first morning after the Sabbath
at the sepulcher where Jesus was buried?**
As the women approached the sepulcher,
"they said among themselves,
Who shall roll us away the stone from the door of the sepulcher?
And when they looked,
they saw that the stone was rolled away:
for it was very great.
And entering into the sepulcher,
they saw a young man [an angel] sitting on the right side,
clothed in a long white garment;
and they were affrighted.
And [the young man] saith unto [the women],
Be not affrighted:
Ye seek Jesus of Nazareth, which was crucified:
behold the place where they laid him.
But go your way, tell his disciples and Peter
that he goeth before you into Galilee:
there shall ye see him, as he said unto you."
(Mark 16:3/7)

168
Why did the young man [the angel]
in the sepulcher where Jesus was buried
single out Peter from Jesus' disciples
to the women who came to the sepulcher?
Three times Peter denied knowing Jesus
after Jesus was arrested.
"And Peter went out [from the hall of the high priest's house],
and wept bitterly."
(Matthew 26, Mark 14, Luke 22 & John 13)
Peter was distraught and grieved over denying Jesus,
but Jesus was eager to forgive Peter
and wanted Peter to know that was still a disciple.
On the occasion of the third meeting
of the disciples with Jesus,
after He arose from the dead,
Jesus asked Peter three times,
using his given name of Simon,
saying, "Simon, son of Jonas,
loveth thou me more than these [other disciples]?"
And three times Peter answered, "Yea, Lord."
(John 21:15/17)

169

Where in the Bible does the word 'Apocalypse' appear?
The word 'Apocalypse' does not appear in the Bible.
An "apocalypse' is a revelation or prophetic disclosure.

170

In which book of the Bible
are the last words of Jesus Christ recorded?
The last words of Jesus Christ
are in the Book of Revelation.
(Revelation 1:8,11 & 18/20, 2:1/29, 3:1/22, 16:15,
22:7, 12/13, 16 & 20)

171

How many people did Jesus raise from the dead?
The Bible records Jesus raising three people from the dead.
He raised of a synagogue ruler's daughter
(Matthew 9:18/26, Mark 5:22/24 & 5:35/43 & Luke 8:41/41 & 49/56),
He raised a widow's son at Nain (Luke 7:11/18),
and He raised Lazarus (John 11:17/46).

172

**What was the occasion when Jesus fed
five thousand from a boy's five loaves and two fishes?**
Jesus fed five thousand after being told
that John the Baptist had been beheaded by Herod Antipas.
"When Jesus heard of it,
he departed thence by ship into a desert place apart [or alone]:
and when the people had heard thereof,
they followed him on foot out of the cities.
And Jesus went forth, and saw a great multitude, and was
moved with compassion toward them, and healed their sick.
And when it was evening, [Jesus'] disciples came to him, saying,
This is a desert place, and the [hour is late];
send the multitude away,
that they may go into the villages, and buy themselves victuals.
But Jesus said unto [the disciples],
They need not depart; give ye them [food] to eat.
And they [said] unto [Jesus],
We have here but five loaves, and two fishes.
[And Jesus] said, Bring them hither to me.
And he commanded the multitude to sit down on the grass,
and took the five loaves, and the two fishes,
and looking up to heaven, he blessed, and brake,
and gave [them] to his disciples, and the disciples to the multitude.
And they did all eat, and were filled:
and they took up of the fragments that
remained twelve baskets full.
And they that had eaten were about five thousand men,
beside women and children."
(Matthew 14:15/ 21, Mark 6:30/44, Luke 9:10/17 & John 6:1/13)

173
What was the occasion when Jesus fed
four thousand from seven loaves and a few fishes?

After feeding the five thousand, Jesus again "departed
into the coasts of Tyre and Sidon."
(Matthew 15:21)
He went into Phoenicia for a brief period of seclusion.
"And Jesus departed from thence,
and came nigh unto the sea of Galilee;
and went up into the mountain, and sat down there.
And great multitudes came unto him, having with them
those that were lame, blind, [mute], maimed, and many others,
and cast them down at Jesus' feet; and [Jesus] healed them:
Inasmuch that the multitude wondered, when they saw
the [mute] to speak, the maimed to be whole, the lame to walk,
and the blind to see: and they glorified the God of Israel."
(Matthew 15:29/31)
Many Gentiles were apparently among the great multitude.
"Then Jesus called his disciples unto him, and said,
I have compassion on the multitude, because they continue
with me now three days, and have nothing to eat:
and I will not send them away fasting, lest they faint in the way.
And his disciples [said] unto him,
Whence should we have so much bread in the wilderness,
as to fill so great a multitude?
And Jesus saith unto them, How many loaves have ye?
And they said, Seven and a few fishes.
And [Jesus] commanded the multitude to sit down on the ground.
And he took the seven loaves and the fishes, and gave thanks,
and brake them, and gave to his disciples,
and the disciples to the multitude.
And they did all eat, and were filled: and
they took up of the broken meat that was left seven baskets full.
And they that did eat were four thousand men,
beside women and children."
(Matthew 15:32/38 & Mark 7:31 / 8:10)

174

Where was the house of Andrew and Peter?
"Philip was of Bethsaida, the city of Andrew and Peter."
(John 1:44)
"Jesus taught in the synagogue at Capernaum.
"And forthwith, when they were come out of the synagogue,
they entered into the house of Simon [Peter] and Andrew,
with James and John."
(Mark 1:21 & 29)
The house of Simon and Andrew was apparently not far from
the synagogue at Capernaum. Both Bethsaida and Capernaum
were on the northeast shore of the Sea of Galilee.
James and John, sons of Zebedee,
are also thought to have lived in this area.

175

**What are the names of the twelve pearl gates to the great city,
holy Jerusalem that shall descend out of heaven from God?**
Each gate has the name of one of the twelve tribes of Israel.
On the north side, from the east side unto the west side,
Levi, Judah, and Reuben;
on the west side, from the north side unto the south side,
Naphtali, Asher, and Gad;
on the south side, from the west side unto the east side,
Zebulun, Issachar, and Simeon;
and on the east side, from the south side unto the north side,
Dan, Benjamin, and Joseph.
(Ezekiel 48 & Revelation 21:12)

176

**What things of twelve are mentioned
in chapter 21 of the Book of Revelation?**
Twelve gates, twelve angels, twelve tribes of the children of Israel,
twelve foundations, twelve apostles of the Lamb,
twelve thousand furlongs, and twelve pearls
are mentioned in chapter 21 of the Book of Revelation.
(Revelation 21:12, 14, 16 & 21)

177

How will Jesus Christ come back to earth from heaven?
"While they [Jesus' apostles] beheld,
[Jesus] was taken up;
and a cloud received him out of their sight.
And while they looked steadfastly toward heaven
as [Jesus] went up, behold,
two men [angels] stood by them in while apparel;
Which also said, Ye men of Galilee,
why stand ye gazing up into heaven?
this same Jesus, which is taken up from you into heaven,
shall so come in like manner
as ye have seen him go into heaven."
(Acts 1:9/11)

178

**Who was the synagogue ruler
whose daughter was raised from the dead?**
The ruler of the synagogue
whose daughter was raised from the dead was Jairus.
(Mark 5:22 & Luke 8:41)

179

Where was Jesus betrayed and arrested?
Jesus was betrayed by Judas and arrested
at the garden of Gethsemane [an olive press]
east of Jerusalem at the foot of the mount of Olives.
"Then cometh Jesus with [his disciples]
unto a place called Gethsemane,
and saith unto his disciples,
Sit ye here, while I go and pray yonder."
"And [soon thereafter], lo,
Judas, one of the twelve, came,
and with him a great multitude with swords and staves,
from the chief priests and elders of the people."
(Matthew 26:36 & 47, Mark 12:32 & 43 & John 18:1)

180

Will there always be wars on the earth?

No. When Jesus Christ comes back to earth
as King of kings, and as Lord of lords,
"He shall judge [or rule] among the nations,
and shall rebuke many people:
and they shall beat their swords into plowshares,
and their spears into pruninghooks:
nation shall not lift up sword against nation,
neither shall they learn war any more."
(Isaiah 2:4 & Micah 4:3)

181

Who shall receive the crown of life?

The crown of life is also called the suffer's crown
and the crown of faithfulness.
"Blessed is the man that endureth temptation [of the devil]:
for when he is tried, he shall receive the crown of life,
which the lord hath promised to them that love him."
(James 1:12)
"Fear none of those things which thou shalt suffer: behold,
the devil shall cast some of you in prison, that ye may be tried,
and ye shall have tribulation ten days [or for a short duration]:
be thou faithful unto death,
and I [Jesus Christ] will give thee the crown of life."
(Revelation 2:10)

182

Who shall receive the watcher's crown?

The watcher's crown is also called the crown of righteousness.
Paul said, "There is laid up for me a crown of righteousness,
which the Lord, the righteous judge, shall give to me at that day:
and not me only, but unto all them also
that love [and watch for] his appearing."
(II Timothy 4:8)

183
Who shall receive the runner's crown?
The runner's crown is also called an incorruptible crown.
"Know ye not that they which run in a race run all,
but one receiveth the prize?
So run, that ye may obtain.
And every man that striveth for the mastery
is temperate [or has self-control] in all things.
Now they do it to obtain a corruptible crown;
but we an incorruptible.
I [Paul] therefore so run, not as uncertainly;
so fight I, not as one that beateth the air:
But I keep under my body, and bring it into subjection:
lest that by any means,
when I have preached to others,
I myself should be a castaway [for crowns]."
(I Corinthians 9:24/27)

184
Who shall receive the shepherd's crown?
The shepherd's crown is also called a crown of glory.
"The elders which are among you I [Peter] exhort,
who am also an elder,
and a witness of the suffering of Christ,
and also a partaker of the glory that shall be revealed:
Feed the flock of God which is among you,
taking oversight thereof,
not by constraint, but willingly;
not for filthy lucre, but of a ready mind;
Neither as being lords over God's heritage,
but being examples to the flock.
And when the chief Shepherd [Jesus Christ] shall appear,
ye shall receive a crown of glory that fadeth not away.
(I Peter 5:1/4)

185
Who is the good shepherd?
Jesus said,
"I am the good shepherd, and know my sheep,
and am known of [my sheep].
As the Father knoweth me,
even so know I the Father:
and I lay down my life for the sheep.
And other sheep I have,
which are not of this fold:
them also must I bring,
and they shall hear my voice;
and there shall be one fold,
and one shepherd.
Therefore doth my Father love me,
because I lay down my life,
that I may take it up again."
(John 10:14/17)

186
What is the soul winner's crown?
The soul winner's crown
is also called a crown of rejoicing.
"The fruit of the righteous is a tree of life;
and he that winneth souls is wise."
(Proverbs 11:30)
"And they that be wise shall shine
as the brightness of the firmament;
and they that turn many to righteousness
as the stars for ever and ever."
(Daniel 12:3)
"For what is our hope, or joy, or crown of rejoicing?
Are not even ye in the presence of our Lord Jesus Christ
at his coming?"
(I Thessalonians 2:19)

187

What does the Bible say about God creating the world?
"In the beginning
God created the heaven and the earth."
(Genesis 1:1)
"All things were made by [God];
and without [God)]
was not any thing made that was made."
(John 1:3)
"The heavens declare the glory of God;
and the firmament showeth his handiwork."
(Psalm 19:1)
"He [God] hath made every thing beautiful in his time:
also he hath set [eternity] in their heart,
so that no man can find out the work
that God maketh from the beginning to the end."
(Ecclesiastes 3:11)
There are many other references in the Bible
to God as the Creator.
"[Even] scoffers, walking after their own lusts,
[acknowledge creation, saying],
Where is the promise of [Jesus'] coming?
for since the fathers fell asleep, all things continue
as they were from the beginning of the creation."
(II Peter 3:3/4)

187=8

Will the Jerusalem of this world be replaced?
Yes, it will be replaced by a new Jerusalem.
"And I John saw the holy city, new Jerusalem,
coming down from God out of heaven,
prepared as a bride adorned for her husband."
(Revelation 21:2)

189

What were Jude's warnings and exhortations to Christians for the end time?

"Beloved, remember ye the words which were spoken before
of the apostles of our Lord Jesus Christ;
How that they told you there should be mockers in the last time,
who should walk after their own ungodly lusts.
These be they who [cause division], [and are worldly],
having not the Spirit.
But ye, beloved, building up yourselves on your holy faith,
praying in the Holy Ghost,
Keep yourselves in the love of God,
looking for the mercy of our Lord Jesus Christ
unto eternal life."
(Jude 1:17/21)

190

Will there be an end of the world?

Yes, but it will be replace by a new world.
Jesus said,
"This gospel of the kingdom shall be preached
in all the world for a witness unto all nations;
and then shall the end come."
(Matthew 24:14)
The day of the Lord will come as a thief in the night;
in the which the heavens shall pass away
with a great noise,
and the elements shall melt with fervent heat,
the earth also and the works that are therein
shall be burned up."
(II Peter 3:10)
"And I saw a new heaven and a new earth:
for the first heaven and the first earth
[shall pass] away;
and there shall be no more sea."
(Revelation 21:1)

191
Will there always be death?
No. Death is a consequence of sin,
and is an enemy of God and man.
All enemies of God and man
shall be subdued to Jesus Christ.
"The last enemy that shall be destroyed is death."
(I Corinthians 15:26)
"And death and hell [shall be] cast into the lake of fire.
This is the second death."
(Revelation 20:14)
"Blessed and holy is he that hath part in the first resurrection
[the rapture of believers]:
on such the second death hath no power,
but they shall be priests of God and of Christ,
and shall reign with him a thousand years."
(Revelation 20:6)

192
How can man be saved from the second death?
"Whosoever
shall call upon the name of [Jesus Christ] the Lord
shall be saved."
Jesus said,
"Verily, verily, I say unto you,
He that heareth [meaning accepts] my word,
and believeth on [God the Father] that sent me,
hath everlasting life, and shall not come into condemnation;
but is [already] passed from death unto life [eternal].
(John 5:24)

193
Where was Jesus crucified?
Jesus was crucified outside the walls of Jerusalem
at "a place called Golgotha, ..., a place of a skull."
(Matthew 27:32/35 & John 19:16/17)

194
Who carried Jesus' cross
from the Jerusalem gate to Golgotha?
"As they came out [of Jerusalem],
they found a man of Cyrene, Simon by name:
him [the governor's soldiers]
compelled to bear [Jesus'] cross."
(Matthew 27:32 & Luke 23:26)

195
Who was one of Paul's first converts from the Roman rulers?
Sergius Paulas,
a prudent man who was proconsul of Cyprus,
called for Barnabas and Saul [Paul],
and desired to hear the word of God.
(Acts 13:7)
But Elymas, the sorcerer ... withstood them,
seeking to turn away [Sergius Paulas] from the faith.
(Acts 13:8)
"Thus Saul [who is also called Paul],
filled with the Holy Ghost, set his eyes on [Elymas],"
and blinded him.
(Acts 13:9/11)
"Then [Sergius Paulas], when he saw what was done,
believed, being astonished at the doctrine of the Lord."
(Acts 13:12)

196
Who was the sorcerer at Paphos who was a false prophet?
"When [Paul and Barnabas and John Mark]
had gone through the isle [of Cyprus] unto Paphos,
they found a certain sorcerer, a false prophet, a Jew,
whose name was Barjesus."
(Acts 13:6)
His name by interpretation was Elymas.
(Acts 13:8)

197
What was Simeon's prayer when he saw the child Jesus?
"And, behold, there was a man in Jerusalem,
whose name was Simeon; [a just and devout man],
waiting for the consolation of Israel:
and the Holy Ghost was upon him.
And it was revealed unto him by the Holy Ghost,
that he should not see death,
before he had seen the Lord's Christ.
And he came by the Spirit into the temple:
and when the parents brought in the child Jesus,
to do for him after the custom of the law,
Then took he him up in his arms,
and blessed God, and [prayed]:
Lord, now lettest thou thy servant depart in peace [Nunc dimittis],
according to thy word:
For mine eyes have seen thy salvation,
Which thou hast prepared before the face of all people;
A light to lighten the Gentiles,
and the glory of thy people Israel."
(Luke 2:25/32)

198
What is Maundy or Holy Thursday?
"Mandatum novum do vobis ut diligatis invicem sicut dilexi vos."
"A new commandment I give unto you,
That ye love one another; as I have loved you."
(John 13:34)
Maundy Thursday is when Jesus
washed the feet of His disciples
on the evening of the Lord's last supper.
Jesus, as our High Priest in heaven,
cleanses us [washes our feet]
of our sins from walking in the world.
(John 13:1/20)

199
How can false teachers be discerned?
"There were false prophets … among the people [of old],
even as there shall be false teachers among you [in the world],
who privily [or secretly] bring in damnable heresies,
even denying the Lord [Jesus Christ] that bought them
[by shedding His blood and dying on the cross],
and bring upon themselves swift destruction."
(II Peter 2:1)
"Beloved [believers], believe not every spirit [of man],
but try [or examine] the spirits whether they are of God:
because many false prophets are gone out into the world."
(I John 4:1)
"Hereby know ye the Spirit of God:
Every spirit that confesseth
that Jesus Christ is come in the flesh is of God:
And every spirit that confesseth not
that Jesus Christ is come in the flesh
is not of God: and this is that spirit of antichrist,
whereof ye have heard that it should come;
and even now already is it in the world."
(I John 4:2/3)

200
Will the Lord judge false teachers?
"Woe unto [false teachers]! for they have gone the way of Cain,
and ran greedily after the error of Balaam for reward,
and perished in the [rebellion] of Korah."
(Jude 1:11)
"Enoch …, the seventh from Adam,
prophesied of these [false teachers], saying,
Behold, the Lord cometh with ten thousands of his saints,
To execute judgment upon all, and to convince all
that are ungodly among them of their ungodly deeds
which they have ungodly committed, and of all their [harsh words]
which ungodly sinners have spoken against [the Lord]."
(Jude 1:14/15)

201
Who will fight the war in heaven?
"There was war in heaven:
Michael and his angels fought against the dragon [Satan];
and the dragon fought and his angels, and prevailed not;
neither was their place found any more in heaven.
And the great dragon was cast out, that old serpent,
called the Devil, and Satan,
which deceiveth the whole world:
he was cast out into the earth,
and his angels were cast out with him."
(Revelation 12:7/9)

202
How are men of faith to grow in grace?
Peter gave us specific instructions of how to grow in grace.
"Giving all diligence, add to your faith virtue;
and to virtue knowledge;
And to knowledge temperance;
and to temperance patience;
and to patience godliness;
And to godliness brotherly kindness;
and to brotherly kindness charity [love]."
(II Peter 1:5/7)
These are progressive characteristics,
and each is perquisite to the next.
The objective of growing in grace is to love one another.
Jesus said,
"By this shall all men know that ye are my disciples,
if ye have love one to another."
(John 13:34/35, 15:12 & 17, Romans 13:8, I Thessalonians 4:9,
I Peter 1:22, I John 3:11 & 23, 47 & 11/12 & II John 1:5)
Growing in grace is what Paul meant when he wrote, saying,
"Wherefore, my beloved, …,
work out your own salvation with fear and trembling."
(Philippians 2:12)

203
When will Satan be cast out into the earth?
Satan will be cast out into the earth
at the mid-point of the Tribulation period.
"And when the dragon [sees] that he [is] cast unto the earth,
he [will persecute] the woman [Israel]
which brought forth the man child."
(Revelation 12:13)
"And the woman [Israel] [will flee] into the wilderness,
where she hath a place [Petra] prepared of God,
that they should feed her there
a thousand, two-hundred and threescore [1,260] days
[during the last half of the Tribulation period]."
(Revelation 12:6)
"And the dragon was wroth with the woman [Israel],
and went to make war with the remnant of her seed,
which keep the commandments of God [the Jews],
and have the testimony of Jesus Christ [believers]."
(Revelation 12:17)

204
**'Every promise of the Bible is mine,
every chapter, every verse, every line.'
Is this a quote from the Bible?**
No, this is not a quote from the Bible
and this is not true.
Every promise of the Bible is not mine.
Promises in the Bible
are for different people at different times.
Promises to Israel are not promises to the Church,
and promises to the Church are not promises to Israel.

205
**What does the Bible say shall happen
to the nations of the world?**
The Bible says, "The kingdoms of this world
[shall] become the kingdoms of our Lord, and of his Christ;
and he shall reign for ever and ever
as Lord of lords, and King of kings."
(Revelation 11:15 & Matthew 17:14)
This happens
after the seventh angel sounds the seventh trumpet.
(Revelation 8:6 & 11:15)
For the unbelieving world, this will be the third 'woe.'
(Revelation 11:14)

206
**Why does the Bible say that the kingdom of Jesus Christ
will last for a thousand years
and also say that there shall be no end of His kingdom?**
The Millennial kingdom of Jesus Christ
shall be here on earth.
"Then cometh the end [of the world], when [Jesus Christ]
shall have delivered up the kingdom to God, even the Father;
when he shall put down all rule and all authority and power
[of the kings and lords of the nations].
(I Corinthians 15:24)
"And when all things shall be subdued unto [Jesus Christ],
then shall the Son also himself be subject unto [God the Father]
that put all things under [God the Son],
that God may be all in all."
(I Corinthians 15:28)
The kingdom of Jesus Christ shall never end,
but will continue for ever and ever
in a place Jesus Christ has prepared for believers.
(John 14:3)

207

What does the Bible say about
the Lord's two witnesses during the Tribulation period?

After the first half or forty-two months of the Tribulation period,
"[Jesus Christ] will give power unto [his] two witnesses,
and they shall prophesy
[during the last half of the Tribulation period for]
a thousand two hundred and threescore days,
clothed in sackcloth."
(Revelation 11:3)
"These [two witnesses] have power to shut heaven,
that it rain not in the days of their prophecy:
and have power over waters to turn them to blood,
and to smite the earth with all plagues,
as often as they will."
(Revelation 11:6)
"And when they shall have finished their testimony,
[Satan] shall make war against them and kill them.
And their dead bodies shall lie in the street of [Jerusalem].
And [all the people of the world]
shall see their dead bodies three days and a half,
and shall not suffer their dead bodies to be put in graves.
And they that dwell upon the earth shall rejoice over them,
and make merry, and shall send gifts one to another;
because these two prophets tormented them ....
And after three days and a half
the spirit of life from God [shall enter] into them,
and they [shall stand] upon their feet;
and great fear [shall fall] upon them which [will have seen] them.
And they [shall hear] a great voice from heaven
saying unto them, Come up hither.
And they [shall ascend] up to heaven in a cloud
and their enemies [shall behold] them."
(Revelation 11:7/12)
"And the same hour [will] there [be] a great earthquake."
(Revelation 11:13)
This will be the second 'woe.'

208
Why do some Christians believe that we are now living in the Millennial kingdom of Jesus Christ?
A primary reason that some Christians believe
that we are now living in the Millennial kingdom of Jesus Christ
is that Jesus said,
"Behold, the kingdom of God is within you."
(Luke 17:21)
They also believe that the meaning of a thousand years
is not specific but instead means innumerable years.

209
How did Paul describe the kingdom of God?
Paul said,
"The kingdom of God is not meat and drink;
but righteousness, and peace, and joy in the Holy Ghost.
(Romans 14:17)

210
What is the difference between the kingdom of God within you and the Millennial kingdom of Jesus Christ?
The kingdom of God within you is the
righteousness, and peace, and joy of the Holy Ghost
that God gives to whosoever believeth in him.
Jesus said,
"Peace I leave with you, my peace I give unto you."
(John 14:27)
The Millennial kingdom of Jesus Christ
is the kingdom that Jesus Christ establishes
here on earth
at His second coming,
to reign as Lord of lords, and as King of kings.
(Isaiah 9:6/7 & Revelation 20:6)

211
Why will the kings of the nations
give their power and strength to the Antichrist
during the Tribulation period?
The kings of the nations
"shall give their power and strength unto the beast [the Antichrist]."
(Revelation 17:13)
"For God hath put in their hearts to fulfill his will,
and to agree, and give their kingdom unto the beast,
until the words of God shall be fulfilled."
(Revelation 17:17)

212
What will be the purpose of the battle at Armageddon?
The battle at Armageddon,
which will be led by the Satan indwelled Antichrist,
will be against Jerusalem and all Israel,
but the real purpose will be to kill Jesus
Christ at His second coming.
"I [John] saw the beast, and the kings of the earth,
and their armies, gathered together to make war against him
that sat on the horse [Jesus Christ], and against his army."
(Revelation 19:19)

213
What does the Bible say about an angel
flying in the midst of heaven during the Tribulation period?
"I [John] saw the seven angels which stood before God;
and to them were given seven trumpets."
(Revelation 8:2)
"And I [John] saw another angel fly in the midst of heaven,
having the everlasting gospel to preach
unto them that dwell on the earth,
and to every nation, and kindred, and tongue, and people.
Saying with a loud voice, Fear God, and give glory to him;
for the hour of his judgment is come: and worship him that made
heaven, and earth, and the sea, and the fountains of waters."
(Revelation 14:6/7)

214
What is the most prominent number in the Book of Revelation?

The number 'seven' is the most prominent number
in the Book of Revelation.
The number 'twelve' is also significant
in the Book of Revelation.

215
How does the Bible group the judgments in the Book of Revelations?

The judgments in the Book of Revelation
are grouped as:
the seven seals (Revelation 6:1 / 8:1),
the seven trumpets (Revelation 8:2 / 11:19),
and the seven bowls or vials (Revelation 15:1 / 16:21).

216
What does the Bible say about the mark of the beast?

"If any man worship the beast [Antichrist] and his image,
and receive ... [the] mark [of the beast]
in his forehead, or in his hand.
The same shall drink of the wine of the wrath of God,
which is poured out without mixture
into the cup of his indignation;
and he shall be tormented with fire and brimstone
in the presence of the holy angels,
and in the presence of the Lamb:
And the smoke of their torment
ascendeth up for ever and ever:
and they have no rest day nor night,
who worship the beast and his image,
and whosoever receiveth the mark of his name."
(Revelation 14:9/11)

217
Who are the 144,000 sealed in their foreheads in Revelation 7:1/8?
The 144,000 include 12,000
from each of the twelve tribes of Israel:
Judah, Reuben, Gad, Asher, Naphtali, Manasseh,
Simeon, Levi, Issachar, Zebulun, Joseph, & Benjamin.
These are sealed for protection and hidden
during the Tribulation period
to preserve a remnant of Israel.
These shall stand on mount Sion [the mount of Olives]
with Jesus Christ when He comes again.
"And I [John] looked, and, lo,
a Lamb [Jesus Christ] stood on mount Sion,
and with him an hundred forty and four thousand,
having his Father's name written in their foreheads."
(Revelation 14:1)

218
Who are in the 'great multitude' of Revelation 7:9?
"After this [after the 144,000 are sealed]
I [John] beheld, and, lo,
a great multitude which no man could number,
of all nations, and kindreds, and people, and tongues,
stood before the throne and before the Lamb,
clothed with white robes, and palms in their hands."
(Revelation 7:9)
The 'great multitude' includes the saved of all ages
through the church age,
worshiping before the throne in heaven.
(Revelation 7:13/17)
Because the 'great multitude' could not be numbered,
it does not represent the 144,000.
Some belief that the 144,000 preach the gospel
and that the 'great multitude'
represents all those who come to Jesus Christ
as a result of their preaching.

219

**After the rapture of the saved of all ages,
why will God send a strong delusion
to those who believed not?**
"Because they received not the love of the truth,
that they might be saved.
And for this cause
God shall send them strong delusion,
that they should believe a lie:
That they all might be damned
[at the great white throne judgment]
who believed not the truth,
but had pleasure in unrighteousness."
(II Thessalonians 2:10/12)
The Antichrist will be the great delusion.
He will "exalt himself above all that is called God."
(II Thessalonians 2:3/10)

220

What should Christians be ready always to do?
The Bible tells Christians to "sanctify [or set apart]
the Lord God in your hearts:
and [to] be ready always
to give an answer to every man that asketh you
a reason of the hope that is in you
with meekness and fear [or reverence]."
(I Peter 3:15)
The hope that Christians have in them
is that:
Jesus Christ is coming again
to take them to heaven to be with Him for ever.

221
What qualifications does the Bible set forth for a bishop?
A bishop is an overseer who has spiritual oversight.
In many churches,
this position is the pastor of the church.
"A bishop … must be blameless,
the husband of one wife, vigilant [temperate],
sober [minded], of good behavior,
given to hospitability, apt [able] to teach;
Not given to wine, no striker [not violent],
not greedy of filthy lucre [money];
but patient, not a brawler, not covetous;
One that ruleth well his own house,
having his children in subjection
with all gravity [reverence];
(For if a man know not how to rule his own house,
how shall he take care of the church of God?)
Not a novice …
[and of] a good report of them
which are without [the church]."
(I Timothy 3:2/7)

222
What qualifications does the Bible set forth for a deacon?
A deacon is an administrative servant.
"Deacons must be grave [reverent],
not double-tongued, not given to much wine,
not greedy of filthy lucre [money];
Holding the mystery of the faith in a pure conscience.
[proven and found blameless before serving].
Even so must their wives be grave [reverent],
not slanderers, sober, faithful in all things.
Let the deacons be the husbands one wife,
ruling their children and their own house well."
(I Timothy 3:8/12)

223
What did Paul say about his living and dying?
Paul said,
"For me to live is Christ, and to die is gain."
(Philippians 1:21)

224
Are believers to hate their enemies?
Jesus said,
"Ye have heard that it hath been said,
Thou shalt love thy neighbour, and hate thine enemy.
But I [Jesus Christ] say unto you,
Love your enemies, bless them that curse you,
do good to them that hate you,
and pray for them which despitefully use you, and persecute you;
That ye may be the children of your Father
which is in heaven:
for he maketh his sun to rise on the evil and on the good,
and sendeth rain on the just and on the unjust."
(Matthew 5:43/45)

225
Are believes to return evil for evil?
"Recompense to no man evil for evil.
[Instead] provide things honest in the sight of all men."
(Romans 12:17)
"See that none render evil for evil unto any man;
but ever follow that which is good,
both among yourselves [believers], and to all men."
(I Thessalonians 5:15)

226
Are believers to judge the faults of others?
Jesus said, "Judge not, that ye be not judged.
For with what judgment ye judge, ye shall be judged:
and with what measure ye mete, it shall
be measured to you again."
(Matthew 7:1/2)

227
How is the Bible profitable?
"All scripture is given by inspiration of God,
and is profitable for doctrine, for reproof,
for correction, for instruction and righteousness:
That the man of God may be perfect,
thoroughly furnished unto all good works."
(II Timothy 3:16/17)

228
Who were the four people in the Bible
whose birth was announced before they were conceived?
Isaac to Sarah (Genesis 18:1/16,
Samson to the unnamed wife of Manoah (Judges 13:2/24,
John the Baptist to Elizabeth (Luke 1:13,
and Jesus to Mary (Luke 1:30/33)

229
What is the difference between the
first and the second death?
The first death is death of the body;
the second death is death of the soul and the body
in the lake of fire.
"Death and hell [shall be] cast into the lake of fire.
This is the second death."
(Revelation 20:14)
Jesus said, "Fear not them which kill the body,
but are not able to kill the soul: but rather fear him
which is able to destroy both soul and body in hell."
(Matthew 10:28)
"Blessed and holy is he that hath part in the first resurrection
[of believers' bodies and their rapture to heaven]:
on such the second death hath no power."
(Revelation 20:6)
"He that hath an ear,
let him hear what the Spirit saith unto the churches;
He that overcometh shall not be hurt of the second death."
(Revelation 2:11)

230
Will the day of the Lord come as a thief in the night?
The day of the Lord will come as a thief in the night
upon nonbelievers, but it will not overtake believers.
"[Believers] know perfectly well that the day of the Lord
so cometh as a thief in the night.
But ye, brethren, are not in darkness,
that that day should overtake you as a thief.
Ye are all the children of light, and children of the day:
we are not of the night, nor of darkness."
(I Thessalonians 5:2 & 4/5)
The Bible oftentimes makes a distinction between
believers as you and nonbelievers as them.

231
What will happen to the heavens when the Lord comes?
"The day of the Lord will come as a thief in the night;
in the which [or in that day] the heavens
shall pass away with a great noise,
and the elements shall melt with fervent heat,
the earth also and the works that are therein shall be burned up."
(II Peter 3:10)
This speaks of the time just before the
great white throne judgment.

232
Who or what is the bride of Christ?
The bride of Christ is that great city, the holy Jerusalem,
and in her are the saved of all ages.
"There came unto me [John] one of the seven angels
which had the seven vials full of the seven last plagues,
and talked with me, saying, Come hither,
I will shew thee the bride, the Lamb's wife.
And he carried me away in the spirit to a great and high mountain,
and shewed me that great city, the holy Jerusalem,
descending out of heaven from God."
(Revelation 21:9/10)
The bride of Christ includes the church, but is more than the church.

233
What are the three great days in the God's plan?
The three great days in God's plan are
Man's Day, the Lord's Day and the Day of Jehovah.
Man's day extends from Adam to Armageddon.
(Titus 2:14 & I Peter 2:9)
The Lord's day extends from
the second coming of Jesus Christ at Armageddon
to the time of the great white throne judgment
when all things shall be subdued and put under Jesus Christ's rule.
(I Corinthians 15:24 & Revelation 17:14 & 20:1/9)
The day of Jehovah, or eternity, extends from
the great white throne judgment to eternity and never ends.
(I Corinthians 15:27/28, Zechariah 14:20 & Revelation 21:2)

234
What three groups are named as coming with Jesus Christ at His second coming to earth?
All the saints, the holy angels, and the armies in heaven.
are named as coming with Jesus Christ at His second coming.
Zechariah said, "The Lord my God shall come,
and all the saints with thee [him].
(Zechariah 14:5 and Revelation 19:8)
"[The saints] that are with [Jesus Christ]
are called, and chosen, and faithful."
(Revelation 17:14)
Jesus said, "When the Son of man shall come in his glory,
and all the holy angels with him,
then shall he sit upon the throne of his glory."
(Matthew 25:31)
And "[John] saw heaven opened, and behold a white horse;
and he that sat upon [the horse] was called Faithful and True,
and in righteousness he doth judge and make war.
[This pictures Jesus' second coming to earth.]
And the armies which were in heaven followed him
upon white horses, clothed in fine linen, white and clean."
(Revelation 19:11 & 14)

235
What will happen to the nations after Armageddon?
All the nations shall be gathered
before Jesus Christ
as King of kings and as Lord of lords.
(Matthew 25:32 & I Timothy 6:15)
"And [the Lord] shall set
the sheep on his right hand,
but the goats on the left.
Then shall the King say unto them on his right hand,
Come, ye blessed of my Father,
inherit the kingdom prepared for you
from the foundation of the world."
"Then shall he say also unto them on the left hand,
Depart from me, ye cursed,
into [the] everlasting [lake of] fire,
prepared for the devil and his angels."
(Matthew 25:33/34 & 25:41)
"And it shall come to pass,
that every one that is left of all the nations
which [go] up against Jerusalem [at Armageddon]
shall even go up from year to year
[during the Millennial kingdom of Jesus Christ here on earth]
to worship the King, the Lord of hosts,
and to keep the feast of tabernacles.
And it shall be,
that whosoever will not come up
of all the families [nations] of the earth
unto Jerusalem to worship
the King, the Lord of hosts,
even upon them shall be no rain."
(Zechariah 14:16/17)

236
Who is Gog and what is the land of Magog?
"The word of the Lord came unto [Ezekiel], saying,
Son of man,
set thy face against Gog, the land of Magog,
the chief prince of Meshech and Tubal,
and prophesy against him."
(Ezekiel 38:1)
People who presently inhabit Russia
are direct descendents of Magog, Tubal, and Meshech,
who are great-grandchildren of Japheth,
one of Noah's sons.
(Genesis 10:2)

237
Who will join with Gog in the invasion of Israel?
Persia [now Iran], Ethiopia, and Libya [will join] with
[the great company of Russians];
all of them with shields and helmets:
[and] Gomer [Germany], and all his bands;
the house of Togarmah [Georgians and Armenians]
of the north quarters, and all his bands:
and many people with thee."
(Ezekiel 38:5/6)

238
When will the invasion of Israel by Gog happen?
The Bible says that the invasion of Israel by Gog
will happen in the latter years.
(Ezekiel 38:8)
It could happen before, during, or after
the Tribulation period,
but events following the invasion seem to indicate
that the invasion will happen
before the Tribulation Period.
(Ezekiel 38:8/16)

239
**What will be Gog's purpose for invading Israel
as prophesied in Ezekiel 38?**
"To take a spoil, and to take a prey;
to turn thine hand upon
the desolate places that are now inhabited,
and upon the people that are gathered out of the nations,
which have gotten cattle and goods,
that dwell in the midst of the land."
(Ezekiel 38:12)

240
**What will be God's purpose of Gog invading Israel
as prophesied in Ezekiel 38?**
For God to "magnify [himself], and sanctify [himself];
and [to make himself] known in the eyes of many nations,
[that] they shall know that [He is] the Lord."
(Ezekiel 38:22/23)

241
What will happen when Gog invades Israel?
God will "plead against [Gog, chief prince of Meshech and Tubal]
with pestilence and with blood;
and [God] will rain upon [Gog], and upon his bands,
and upon the many people that are with him,
and [flooding] rain, and great hailstones, fire, and brimstone.
(Ezekiel 38:22 & 39:1)
"And [God] will turn [Gog] back, and leave
but the sixth part of thee."
(Ezekiel 39:2)
God will smite them,
and they shall fall upon the mountains of Israel.
(Ezekiel 39:3/4)
"And God will send a fire on Magog,
and among them that dwell carelessly in the isles:
and they shall know that I am the Lord."
(Ezekiel 39:6)

242
What will be the aftermath of Gog's defeat by God?
"[God] will make [his] holy name known
in the midst of [his] people Israel:
and [He] will not let them
pollute [his] holy name any more."
This will not necessarily be
when Israel recognizes Jesus Christ as the Messiah.
(Ezekiel 39:7)
"Seven months shall the house of Israel
be burying of them,
that they may cleanse the land."
(Ezekiel 39:12)
"And it shall be to them [the children of Israel]
a renown the day that [God] shall be glorified,
saith the Lord God."
(Ezekiel 39:13)

243
To whom was the Book of Hebrews addressed?
Ancient manuscripts say "To Hebrews,"
but the content indicates that the book was addressed
to Jewish Christians who were tempted
to return to Judaism,
in part to avoid Christian persecution.

244
What is the major theme of the Book of Hebrews?
The major theme of the Book of Hebrews
is the superiority of Jesus Christ.
(Hebrews 1:4, 8:6 & 11:4)

245
Who was Joseph of Arimathaea?
"Joseph of Arimathaea [was] an honourable counselor,
which also waited for the kingdom of God.
[He] went in boldly unto Pilate [when Jesus had died],
and [asked for] for the body of Jesus."
(Mark 15:43)
Joseph of Arimathaea was also a disciple of Jesus.
(Matthew 27:57 & John 19:38)
"And he brought fine linen, and took [Jesus] down [from the cross],
and wrapped him in the linen,
and laid him in a sepulcher which was hewn out of a rock,
and rolled a stone unto the door of the sepulcher."
(Mark 15:46)

246
What does the Bible say about Demas?
In Colossians and Philemon, Paul named Demas
as a fellow laborer for the Lord.
"Luke, the beloved physician, and Demas, greet you."
(Colossians 4:14)
Paul wrote,
"There salute thee Epaphras,
my fellow prisoner in Christ Jesus;
Marcus, Aristarchus, Demas, Lucas, my fellow laborers."
(Philemon 1:23/24)
But when Paul was in prison in Rome
during his final days,
Demas abandoned Paul,
and Paul wrote to Timothy, saying,
"For Demas hath forsaken me,
having loved this present world,
and is departed unto Thessalonica;
Crescens to Galatia, Titus unto Dalmatia."
(II Timothy 4:10)

247
What is Dominion theology?
Dominion theology is a view
that a kingdom of Mosaic law
must be established by man over the world
as a prerequisite to Jesus Christ coming back to earth.
Dominion theology is also called Christian Reconstructionism.
This view conflicts with what the Bible says.
The Bible says that Jesus Christ will return to earth
and establish a kingdom to bring about righteousness.
(Revelation 19:11 / 20:4)
Christians are commanded by God to preach the gospel;
not to take dominion of the world.
(Matthew 28:19/20)

248
When will the times of the Gentiles end?
The times of the Gentiles will end
when Jesus returns to the earth
as King of kings and Lord of lords.
Until then, Gentiles will exercise rule
over Jerusalem and the nations.
The Tribulation period known as the time of Jacob's trouble,
which will be the final seven years of the 490 years
determined upon the children of Israel and upon Jerusalem
(Daniel 9:24),
will run concurrent with the last seven years
of the times of the Gentiles.

249
Why are believers not to avenge ourselves
for wrongs others do to us?
"Vengeance is mine, saith the Lord, [and] I will repay."
(Deuteronomy 32:35 & Romans 12:19)

250
Has God abandoned Israel?
Many say that God has abandoned Israel,
but Paul said, "God forbid:
but rather through [Israel's] fall
salvation is come unto the Gentiles,
for to provoke [Israel] to jealousy."
(Romans 11:11)
"Did not Israel know?
First Moses saith,
I will provoke you to jealousy
by them that are no people,
and by a foolish nation I will anger you."
(Deuteronomy 32:21 & Romans 10:19)

251
What do 'hunger' and 'thirst' represent in the Bible?
'Hunger' and 'thirst' represent desire and want.
Jesus said,
"Blessed are they
which do hunger and thirst
after righteousness:
for they shall be filled."
(Matthew 5:6)

252
Who can satisfy man's hunger and thirst?
Jesus alone can satisfy man's hunger and thirst.
Jesus said,
"I am the bread of life."
(John 6:48)
And Jesus said,
"Whosoever drinketh
of the water that I shall give him shall never thirst;
but the water that I give him shall be a well of water
springing up into everlasting life."
(John 4:14)

253
What does the Bible say will come in the last days?
The Bibles says,
"that in the last days perilous times shall come.
For men shall be lovers of their own selves,
covetous, boasters, proud, blasphemers,
disobedient to parents, unthankful, unholy,
without natural affection,
trucebreakers, false accusers, [without self control],
fierce, despisers of those that are good,
traitors, heady, highminded,
lovers of pleasures more than lovers of God;
Having a form of godliness,
but denying the power thereof:
from such turn away."
(II Timothy 3:1/5)

254
Where is a brief history of the Bible?
Bible history is presented in capsule
in the first three verses of the Book of Hebrews
in this manner:
"God, who at sundry times and in divers manners spake
in times past unto the fathers by the prophets,
Hath in these days spoken unto us by his Son [Jesus],
whom he hath appointed heir of all things,
by whom also he made the worlds;
Who being the brightness of [God's] glory,
and the express image of [God's] person,
and upholding all things
by the word of [God's] power,
when he had by himself purged our sins,
sat down on the right hand of the Majesty on high."
(Hebrews 1:1/3)

255

**'For all they that take the sword shall perish with the sword.'
Is this a quote from the Bible?**
Yes. This quote is from Matthew 26:52.
Jesus said this after Peter "drew his sword,
and struck a servant of the high priest's, and smote off his ear."
This is often misquoted as
'They that live by the sword shall die by the sword.'

256

What was the origin of the Protestant churches?
Protestant churches originated with the Protestant Reformation.
The Roman Catholic Church claims to be
a continuation of the Christian church
of which Jesus is the cornerstone
and of which St. Peter was the first bishop.
Protestant churches seceded from the Roman Catholic Church
in protest of certain orthodox doctrines and practices
such as priesthood, who could interpret the scriptures,
grace, and the sacraments.

257

How did Jesus distinguish a wise man from a foolish man?
Jesus said,
"whosoever heareth [understands]
these sayings of mine, and doeth them,
I will liken him unto a wise man, which built his house upon a rock.
And the rain descended, and the floods came,
and the winds blew, and beat upon the house; and it fell not:
for it was founded upon a rock.
And every one that heareth these sayings of mine,
and doeth them not, shall be likened unto a foolish man,
which built his house upon the sand:
And the rain descended, and the floods came,
and the winds blew, and beat upon that house; and it fell:
and great was the fall of it."
(Matthew 7:24/27)

258
How does the Bible describe an atheist?
"The fool hath said in his heart, There is no God.
They are corrupt, they have done abominable works,
there is none that doeth good."
(Psalm 14:1)
"The fool has said in his hear, There is no God.
Corrupt are they, and have done abominable iniquity:
there is none that doeth good."
(Psalm 53:1)
"That which may be known of God is manifest in them;
for God hath shewed it unto them.
For the invisible things of him
from the creation of the world are clearly seen,
being understood by the things that are made,
even his eternal power and Godhead;
so that they are without excuse:
Because that,
when they knew God,
they glorified him not as God,
neither were thankful;
but became vain in their imaginations,
and their foolish heart was darkened."
(Romans 1:19/21)

259
Why are believers to put on the whole armor of God?
"Put on the whole armor of God,
that ye may be able to stand against the wiles of the devil.
For we wrestle not against flesh and blood,
but against principalities,
against powers,
against the rulers of the darkness of this world,
against spiritual wickedness in high places."
(Ephesians 6:11/12)

260
What are some of the signs that Jesus Christ told the Pharisees and Sadducees that they could not discern?

Deception --
"Jesus said unto them,
Take heed that no man deceive you.
For many shall come in my name, saying,
I am Christ;
and shall deceive many."
(Matthew 24:4/5)
Wars and Rumors of Wars --
Jesus said, "Ye shall hear of wars and rumors of wars:
... for all these things must come to pass, but the end is not yet."
(Matthew 24:6/7)
Famine, Pestilence, and Earthquakes --
"and there shall be famines, and pestilence, and earthquakes,
in divers places.
(Matthew 24:7)
Anti-Semitism --
Jesus said,
"Then shall they deliver you up to be afflicted,
and shall kill you: and shall be hated of all nations
for my name's sake."
(Matthew 24:9)
Offenses [or crimes] Against Many --
"And then shall many be offended."
(Matthew 24:10)
Betrayal -- "and [many] shall betray one another."
(Matthew 24:10)
Hatred -- "and [many] shall hate one another."
(Matthew 24:10)
and Absence of Love --
Jesus said, "the love of many shall wax cold."
(Matthew 24:12)
"But he that shall endure unto the end [of his life],
the same shall be saved."
(Matthew 24:13)

261
What happened to the eight writers of the New Testament?
Matthew was slain with a halberd [a battle axe],
Mark was dragged by horses through the streets of Alexandria
until he was dead,
Luke was hanged in an olive tree,
John was thrown into a caldron of boiling oil
and exiled to the Isle of Patmos,
Paul was beheaded,
Jude and Peter were crucified,
and James was battered with a fuller's club.

262
What is Alleluia and where in the Bible does it appear?
Alleluia (and Hallelujah) is an expression of praise to the Lord.
Alleluia appears four times, in the of the Book of Revelation.
(Revelation 19:1, 3, 4 and 6)
Hallelujah does not appear in the Bible.

263
How many people does the Bible say that Paul healed?
The Bible records Paul healing only one person.
"It came to pass, that the father of Publius
lay sick of a fever and of a bloody flux:
to whom Paul entered in, and prayed,
and laid his hands on him, and healed him."
(Acts 28:8)

264
Who did Paul baptize?
Paul said, "I thank God that I baptized none of you,
but Crispus and Gaius.
And I baptized also the household of Stephanas:
besides, I know not whether I baptized any other."
(Acts 1:14 & 16)
"For Christ sent me not to baptize, but to preach the gospel."
(Acts 1:17)

265
What gift is given to every believer to profit all?
"The manifestation of the Spirit is given
to every man [who is a believer] to profit [all]."
(I Corinthians 12:7)

266
What is the fruit of the Spirit?
"The fruit of the Spirit is love,
joy, peace, long-suffering, gentleness,
goodness, faith, meekness, [and] temperance."
(Galatians 5:22/23)

267
Which verses of the Bible describe the mind or attitude of Christ Jesus?
"Let this mind be in you, which was also in Christ Jesus:
Who being in the form of God,
thought it not robbery to be equal with God:
But made himself of no reputation,
and took upon him the form of a servant,
and was made in the likeness of men:
And being found in fashion [or appearance] as a man,
he humbled himself, and became obedient unto death,
even the death of the cross."
(Philippians 2:5/8)

268
Who does the Bible say is a liar?
"Who is a liar but he that denieth that Jesus is the Christ?
He is antichrist,
that denieth the Father and the Son.
(I John 2:22)

269
Why did Jesus Christ give Himself for us?
"[Jesus Christ] gave himself for us,
that he might redeem us from all iniquity,
and purify unto himself a peculiar people,
zealous for good works."
(Titus 2:13/14)
"God commendeth his love toward us, in that,
while we were yet sinners, Christ died for us."
(Romans 5:8)

270
Was there any possible way other than the cross for Jesus Christ to redeem us from our iniquities?
Jesus prayed to God the Father,
"If it were possible, the hour might pass from him.
And he said, Abba, Father, all things are possible unto thee;
take away this cup from me:
nevertheless not what I will, but what thy wilt."
(Mark 14:35/36 & Luke 22:41/42)
Jesus said, "No man cometh unto the Father, but by me."
(John 14:6)

If you have comments about the answers presented,
search the scriptures and send me your succinct answers with KJV Bible verse references at
JerryAdamsQandA@aol.com.

Question

_____

_____?

Answer

_____

_____

_____

_____

_____

_____

_____

_____

_____.

(_____)

Question

_____

_____?

Answer

_____

_____

_____

_____

_____

_____

_____

_____

_____.

(_____)

CHRISTIAN BIBLE CHALLENGE
ANSWERS EVERY CHRISTIAN SHOULD KNOW

OLD TESTAMENT QUESTIONS & ANSWERS

The New Testament is concealed in the Old Testament.

II
**How many books are there
in the King James Version of the Old Testament?**
There are thirty-nine books in the Old Testament.

301
Which book of the Bible is the Book of Faith?
Genesis is the Book of faith,
and Abraham is described as
"the father of all them that believe."
(Romans 4:11)
The eleventh chapter of the Book of Hebrews
lists some Old Testament champions of faith.

302
What is the Pentateuch?
The first five books of the Bible:
Genesis, Exodus, Leviticus, Numbers, and Deuteronomy.

303
**What were the four major events
in the first eleven chapter of Genesis?**
The four major events
in the first eleven chapters of Genesis were
Creation,
the Fall of Man,
Noah and the Flood,
and the Division of the Earth at Babel.
(Genesis 1 / 11)

304
**How does the Bible say
the heavens and the earth came into existence?**
"In the beginning
God created the heavens and the earth."
(Genesis 1:1)
"Let them praise the name of the Lord:
for he commanded,
and they were created."
(Psalm 148:5)

305
What did God create on each of the days
of the creation of the world?
Day One
The Heavens and the Earth, Waters, Light, and Day and Night
Day Two
The Firmament [Heaven]
Day Three
Seas, Land and Vegetation
Day Four
Heavenly Bodies [Sun, Moon and Stars]
Day Five
Animal life of the Sea and the Air
Day Six
Animal Life of the Earth and Man
Day Seven
God rested from all his work of creation
and sanctified the seventh day.
(Genesis 1:1 & 2:3)

306
Who was the first son of Adam and Eve?
Cain was the first son of Adam and Eve.
Cain means 'acquire.'
Eve said,
"I have gotten a man from the Lord."
(Genesis 4:1)

307
Who were Adam and Eve's second and third sons?
The second son of Adam and Eve was Abel,
who was killed by Cain.
Seth was their third son.
From the linage of Seth came Noah, Abraham, David and Jesus.
(Genesis 4:2 & 4:25)

308
How was heaven created?
"And the earth was without form,
and void [without life];
and darkness was upon the face of the deep.
And the Spirit of God moved upon the face of the waters."
(Genesis 1:2)
"God said,
Let there be a firmament in the midst of the waters,
and let it divide the waters from the waters."
And God made the firmament,
and divided the waters which were under the firmament
from the waters which were above the firmament.
And God called the firmament Heaven."
(Genesis 1:6/8)

309
Who are the Hebrews?
Hebrews are people of the Semitic language.
Eber [Heber], a great-grandson of Shem,
refused to participate in the building of the Tower of Babel.
When the language of the people was confounded
(Genesis 1:7/9),
the people of Eber retained the original language
which was then called Eber's language or Hebrew.
Abram was a descendant of Eber.
The term 'Hebrew' first appears in the Bible at Genesis 14:13.
"And there came one that escaped
[from Sodom and Gomorrah],
and told Abram the Hebrew
[that Lot had been taken captive];
for he dwelt in the plain of Mamre the Amorite,
brother of Eshcol, and brother of Aner:
and these were [allies] with Abram."
The Hebrews became known as Israelites and Jews.

310
Why did the Lord have respect unto Abel and his offering, but unto Cain and his offering the Lord had not respect?
"Abel was a keeper of sheep, …
and he brought [an offering] of
the firstlings of his flock and of the fat thereof."
Abel's offering required the shedding of blood.
But "Cain was a tiller of the ground, …
and he brought [an offering] of the fruit of the ground."
Cain's offering did not involve the shedding of blood.
(Genesis 4:2/5)

311
How does Satan cause people to rebel against God?
Satan starts with a lie that there is no truth.
(Genesis 3:1)
Then Satan tells people that God is impersonal.
Satan then convinces people that they can be gods,
and that they shall not surely die
or that they will be reincarnated.
(Genesis 3:4)
Some then get involved with mind-altering consciousness.
Satan then incites people to rebel against God.
Satan also uses other means
to get people to rebel against God.
The Bible says, "Be sober, be vigilant;
because your adversary the devil, as a roaring lion,
walketh about, seeking whom he may devour."
(I Peter 5:8)

312
Who was the first prophet in the Bible to die?
Abel was the first prophet to die.
Abel was referred to by Jesus as a prophet.
(Matthew 23:35 & Luke 11:49/51)
He was murdered by his brother Cain.
(Genesis 4:8)

313
Who responded to God by saying,
"Am I my brother's keeper?"
When God said unto Cain, Where is Abel thy brother?
Cain responded to God by saying,
"I know not: Am I my brother's keeper?"
(Genesis 4:9)

314
In what land did Cain dwell
after he went out from the presence of the Lord?
"Cain went out from the presence of the Lord,
and dwelt in the land of Nod, on the east of Eden."
(Genesis 4:16)

315
Who was the father of all such as handle the harp and organ?
"Jubal [the son of Lamech and Adah] was the father
of all such as handle the harp and organ."
(Genesis 4:21)

316
Who were the two wives of Lamech?
"Lamech took unto him two wives: the name of the one was Adah,
and the name of the other was Zillah."
(Genesis 4:19)

317
Why did Lamech feel that he would be avenged?
"Lamech said unto his wives, Adah and Zillah,
Hear my voice; ye wives of Lamech,
hearken unto my speech:
for I have slain a man to my wounding,
and a young man to my hurt.
If Cain be avenged sevenfold,
truly Lamech seventy and sevenfold."
(Genesis 4:23/24 & 4:15)
This tells of the wickedness state of man before God sent the flood.

318
When did men begin to call upon the name of the Lord?
"To Seth [the third son of Adam and Eve] …
there was born a son; and he called his name Enos:
then began men to call upon the name of the Lord."
(Genesis 4:25/26)

319
Who were the descendents of Adam to Noah?
Adam, Seth, Enos, Cainan, Mahalaleel,
Jared, Enoch, Methuselah,
and Lamech, father of Noah
(Genesis 5:1/31)

320
What did God see when He looked upon the earth?
"And God looked upon the earth,
and, behold, it was corrupt;
for all flesh had corrupted his way upon the earth."
(Genesis 6:12)

321
What was the Bible ancestry from Adam to the flood?

	Year B.C.	Year Born	Son Born	Then Lived	Age at Death	Year *Died	Year B.C.
Adam	4004	0	130	800	930	930	3074
Seth	3874	130	105	782	912	1042	2904
Enos	3769	235	90	815	905	1140	2864
Cainan	3679	325	70	840	910	1235	2769
Mahalaleel	3609	395	65	830	895	1290	2714
Jared	3544	460	162	800	962	1422	2582
Enoch	3382	622	65	300	365	* 987	3017
Methuselah	3317	687	187	782	969	1656	2348
Lamech	3130	874	182	595	777	1651	2353
Noah	2948	1056	**600	350	950	2006	1998
Flood	2348	1656					

* Enoch was taken by God and did not die.   ** Flood
(Genesis 5 & I Chronicles 1:1/4)

322
What happened to Enoch?
"Enoch walked with God: and he was not; for God took him."
(Genesis 5:24 & Hebrews 11:5)

323
Who was the oldest man in the Bible to die?
Methuselah lived longer than any other man in the Bible.
He lived 969 years.
(Genesis 5:27)

324
How did Methuselah die before his grandfather died?
Enoch was Methuselah's grandfather,
and Enoch did not die.
(Genesis 5:24 & Hebrews 11:5)

325
What happened in the year that Methuselah died?
In the same year that Methuselah died, the flood came.
His name meant: When he is dead; judgment!
(Genesis 5:25, 28 & 29 & 7:6)

326
In what year did Methuselah die?
Methuselah died in 2348 B.C., the Year of the Flood.
(Genesis 5)

327
When God decided to destroy man for his wickedness, why was Noah saved?
Because "Noah found grace in the eyes of the Lord."
(Genesis 6:7/8)
The Bible says, "For by grace are ye saved through faith;
and that not of yourselves: it is a gift from God:
Not of works, lest any man should boast."
(Ephesians 2:8/9)

328
Who were the sons of Noah?
Noah's three sons were Shem, Ham, and Japheth.
(Genesis 5:32)

329
Why are the Jews called Semites?
'Semitic' is an adjective derived from Shem,
one of Noah's three sons from whom
Abraham, Isaac and Jacob were descendents.
(Genesis 5:32)
Semites included all peoples who spoke the Semitic language,
but the term 'anti-Semitic' is directed specifically at the Jews.

330
Why did the Lord repent that He made man on the earth?
Because "God saw the wickedness of man
was great in the earth,
and that every imagination of the thoughts of [man's] heart
was only evil continually.
[This] grieved [God] at his heart."
(Genesis 6:5/6)

331
How long was the flood upon the earth?
"The rain was upon the earth forty days and forty nights."
"[Then] the waters prevailed upon the earth
a hundred and fifty days."
(Genesis 7:12 & 7:24)

332
Where did Noah's ark come to rest?
"And [Noah's] ark rested in the seventh month,
on the seventeenth day of the month,
upon the mountains of Ararat."
(Genesis 8:4)

333
Who were the eight people who survived the flood?
Noah, and his three sons, and his wife, and his sons' wives.
(Genesis 8:18)

334
How old was Noah when he died,
and in what year did he die?
Noah died when he was 950 years old,
and he died in 1998 B.C.

335
What sign did God give
that waters would never again flood the earth?
God gave a rainbow as a sign of His promise.
"God said [unto Noah], This is the token of the covenant
which I make between me and you … for perpetual generations:
I do set my bow in the clouds."
(Genesis 9:8/13)

336
How was the earth repopulated after the flood?
"Now these are the generations of the sons of Noah,
Shem, Ham, and Japheth:
and unto them were sons born after the flood."
(Genesis 10:10)
"The families of the sons of Noah,
after their generations, in their nations:
and by these were the nations divided in the earth after the flood."
(Genesis 10:32)

337
How were the lands of the Gentiles divided?
The Bible says, "by these
[the descendents of Noah by their languages]
were the nations divided in the earth after the flood."
(Genesis 10:5, 20 & 32)

338
Who were the descendents of Noah to Abraham?
Noah, Shem, Arphaxad, Salah, Eber, Peleg, Reu,
Serug, Nahor, and Terah, father of Abram
whose name was changed by God to Abraham
(Genesis 10:10/26 & 17:5)

339
Who was Nimrod and what does his name mean?
Nimrod, meaning 'rebel,' was a son of Cush,
a grandson of Ham and a great grandson of Noah.
"He began to be a mighty [man] in the earth."
He was king of Shinar [Mesopotamia].
(Genesis 10:8/10)
Nimrod is associated with the building of the Tower of Babel.
'Land of Nimrod' is used as a synonym for Assyria.

340
Who were the sons of Japeth
and what are the nations they populated?
"The sons of Japheth; Gomer
[Russians, Gauls, Germans, and Britons],
and Magog [Scythians], and Madai [Medes],
and Javan [Greeks], and Tubal [Iberians],
and Meshech [Muscovites], and Tiras [Thracians]."
(Genesis 10:2)
These people populated Asia Minor, Caucasia and Europe.

341
Who were the sons of Ham
and what are the nations they populated?
"The sons of Ham; Cush [Ethiopians], and Mizraim [Egyptians],
and Phut [Lydians], and Canaan [Canaanites]."
(Genesis 10:6)
These people populated Arabia, Egypt, and North Africa.

342

Who were the sons of Shem
and what are the nations they populated?
"The children of Shem; Elam [Elamites or Persians],
and Asshur [Assyrians], and Arphaxad [Chaldeans],
and Lud [Libyians], and Aram [Syrians and Armenians]."
(Genesis 10:22)
These people populated the Middle East.

343

Who built the city of Nineveh?
"Out of [the land of Shinar] went forth Asshur,
and builded Nineveh,
and the city of Rehoboth, and Calah,
and Resen between Nineveh and Calah.
(Genesis 10:11/12)

344

Who was the father of Isaac's wife, Rebekah?
Bethuel was the father of Rebekah.
Bethuel was the eighth child of Nahor, Abraham's brother.
(Genesis 11:29, 22:20/23 & 24:15)

345

Where was Abram when the Lord called him
to leave his country, and his kindred, and his father's house,
and go unto a land that the Lord would show him?
Abram dwelt in Haran when the Lord called him to leave.
"Abram departed,
as the Lord had spoken unto him;
and ... departed out of Haran.
And Abram took Sarai his wife,
and Lot his brother's son ...,
and they went forth into the land of Canaan."
(Genesis 12:4/5)

346
How was Abram saved?
Abram was saved by God's grace.
"[Abram] believed in the Lord;
and [the Lord God] counted it to him for righteousness."
(Genesis 15:6)

347
God changed Abram's name to what?
Abram's name was later changed to Abraham.
(Genesis 17:5)

348
Who was Melchizedek?
Melchizedek, also spelled Melchisedec,
was the high priest of Salem who blessed Abram
after Abram's "slaughter of Chedorlaomer [king of Elam],
and the kings that were with him, at the valley of Shaveh,"
to rescue Lot, who had been taken captive.
(Genesis 14:18/20), Psalm 110:4 &
Hebrews 5:6 & 10, 6:20, 7:1, 10/11, 15, 17 & 21)

349
Was Ishmael a Hebrew?
Abram, the father of Ishmael, was a Hebrew,
but Hagar, the mother of Ishmael was an Egyptian handmaid.
"Hagar bare Abram a son:
and Abram called his son's name, which Hagar bare, Ishmael."
(Genesis 16)
Ishmael became the father of the Arabs,
and as such is not viewed as a Hebrew.
After changing Abram's name to Abraham
and Sarai's name to Sarah, God told Abraham:
"My covenant will I establish with Isaac,
which Sarah shall bear unto thee at this set time in the next year."
(Genesis 17:5 & 21)

350
How many princes did Ishmael beget?
Ishmael was the father of twelve princes
as God promised Abraham.
"As for Ishmael, I have heard thee:
Behold I have blessed him, and will make him fruitful;
twelve princes shall he beget, and I will make him a great nation."
(Genesis 17:20)
Ishmael also had a daughter who married Esau.

351
God's covenant with Abraham was established with whom?
God established His covenant with Isaac and Jacob.
(Genesis 17:21, 26:3, 35:11/12,
I Chronicles 16:17, Psalm 105:10 & Exodus 2:24)

352
Why did the Lord destroy Sodom and Gomorrah?
"Because the cry of Sodom and Gomorrah [was] great,
and because their sin [was] very grievous."
(Genesis 18:20)

353
How did Abraham intercede for Sodom?
"Abraham drew near [to the Lord], and said,
Wilt thou also destroy the righteous with the wicked?"
And the Lord said, "I will not destroy [Sodom]
for [the sake of ten who are righteous]."
(Genesis 18:22/32)
But there were not found ten who were righteous.

354
Who escaped the destruction of Sodom?
Lot and his two daughters escaped the destruction of Sodom.
Lot's wife was brought forth without the city,
but she looked back toward Sodom in defiance of the Lord
and she became a pillar of salt.
(Genesis 19:15/29)

355
Who were the children of Lot's two daughters?
The son of Lot's first-born daughter was Moab,
the father of the Moabites,
and the son of Lot's younger daughter was Ben-ammi,
the father of the children of Ammon.
(Genesis 19:30/38)

356
Who were the descendents of Abraham to Jacob (or Israel)?
Abraham, Isaac, and Jacob, whose name was changed to Israel.
(Genesis 21:1/3, 25:21/26 & 32:28)

357
How old was Abraham when Isaac was born?
"Abraham was a hundred years old,
when his son Isaac was born to him."
(Genesis 21:4)

358
Why did Abraham circumcise his son Isaac?
"Abraham circumcised his son Isaac being eight days old."
(Genesis 21:3)
This was a sign of God's covenant with Abraham
and Abraham's seed in their generations.
(Genesis 17:9/14)

359
How did God test Abraham?
"[God] said [to Abraham],
Take now thy son, thine only son Isaac,
whom thou lovest, and get thee into the land of Moriah;
and offer [Isaac] there for a burnt offering
upon one of the mountains which I will tell thee of."
(Genesis 22:1/2)

360
Why did God tell Abraham to offer Isaac,
Abraham's only son, as a burnt offering?

God told Abraham to offer Isaac as a burnt offering
to test Abraham's fear [reverence and obedience] of God,
and to show that
"God [would] provide himself a lamb for a burnt offering."
(Genesis 22:1/14)
God's promise was fulfilled
when He gave his only begotten Son, Jesus Christ,
that whosoever believeth in him [Jesus Christ]
should not perish, but have everlasting life.
(John 3:16)

361
Why did Abraham send his servant to Abraham's country,
and to his kindred to bring to Canaan a wife unto Isaac,
and forbid his servant from taking Isaac?

Because Abraham did not want Isaac
to be tempted or persuaded to stay in Abraham's country
with his kindred.
"The Lord God of heaven,
which took [Abraham] from [his] father's house,
and from the land of [his] kindred,
and which spake unto [him],
and that sware unto [him],
saying,
Unto thy seed will I give this land;
he [the Lord God] shall send his angel
before [Abraham's servant],
and thou shalt take a wife unto my son from thence.
And if the woman will not be willing to follow thee,
then thou shalt be clear [or released] from this my oath:
only bring [or take] not my son thither [there] again."
(Genesis 24:7/8)

362
Where were Abraham and Sarah buried?
"In a cave of the field of Machpelah before Mamre:
the same is Hebron in the land of Canaan."
(Genesis 23:19 & 25:9/10)

363
Who were the sons of Isaac and Rebekah?
"When [Rebekah's] days to be delivered were fulfilled,
behold, there were twins in her womb.
And the first came out red, all over like a hairy garment;
and they called his name Esau.
And after that came his brother out,
and his hand took hold on Esau's heel;
and his name was called Jacob:
and Isaac was threescore years old when [Rebekah] bare them."
(Genesis 25:24/26)

364
Why did God hate Esau?
The Book of Obadiah explains why God hated Esau.
"Esau despised his birthright."
(Genesis 25:34)
Esau had no regard for the things of God.
He treated the sacred things of God as common.
Esau is described as a profane person.
(Hebrews 12:16)
Unbelief of the gospel is the supreme evil.
"He that despised Moses' law died without mercy
under two or three witnesses.
Of how much sorer punishment, suppose ye,
shall he be thought worthy,
who hath trodden under foot the Son of God,
and hath counted the blood of the covenant,
wherewith he was sanctified, an unholy thing,
and hath done despite unto the Spirit of grace?"
(Hebrews 10:28/29)

365
What was the covenant that God made with Abram?
"The Lord made a covenant with Abram,
saying,
Unto thy seed have I given this land,
from the river of Egypt unto the great river,
the river Euphrates."
(Genesis 15:18)

366
Who were the sons of Abraham?
Ishmael was Abraham's son by Hagar,
the handmaid of Sarai,
and Isaac was Abraham's son by Sarah,
Abraham's wife,
whose name was changed by God
from Sarai to Sarah.
(Genesis 16, 17:15 & 21:3)

367
Ishmael was how many years older than Isaac?
Ishmael was 14 years old when Isaac was born.
(Genesis 16:16 & 21:5)

368
**What did Abraham call the name of the place
where he prepared to offer Isaac, his only son,
as a burnt offering?**
"Abraham called the name of the place
Jehovah-jireh:
as it is said to this day,
In the mount of the Lord
it shall be seen [provided]."
(Genesis 22:14)

369

**For what cause shall a man leave father and mother,
and shall cleave to his wife?**
"God created man … in the image of God created him;
male and female created him.
And God blessed them,
and God said unto them,
Be fruitful, and multiply, and replenish the earth."
(Genesis 1:27/28)
"For this cause shall a man leave father and mother,
and shall cleave to his wife:
and they twain shall be one flesh."
(Genesis 2:24 & Matthew 19:5)

370

Who lied for fear saying his wife was his sister?
Abram told Pharaoh of Egypt
that Sarai was his sister.
(Genesis 12)
Isaac told Abimelech, king of Gerar,
that Rebekah was his sister.
(Genesis 26:6/7)

371

How was Esau related to Ishmael?
Esau married Ishmael's daughter, Mahalath,
and was Ishmael's son-in-law.
(Genesis 28:9)

372

Who was the father of Jacob's wives, Leah and Rachel?
Laban, a brother of Rebekah,
was the father of Leah and Rachel.
(Genesis 29:10, 29:16, 29:25 & 29:28)

373
How was Jacob's name changed to Israel?
Jacob wrestled at Peniel with a man
thought to be God or an angel of God
and prevailed in obtaining God's blessing.
(Genesis 32:24/32)

374
How old was Abraham when he died?
"These [were] the days of the years
of Abraham's life which he lived,
an hundred threescore and fifteen [175] years.
(Genesis 25:7)

375
**What is the second holiest site for the Jews
after the Temple Mount in Jerusalem?**
The Cave of the Patriarchs
or the Cave of Machpelah in Hebron,
where Abraham and Sarah,
Isaac and Rebecca,
and Jacob and Leah
are said to be buried.
(Genesis 23:19, 25:9/10, 35:29, 50:13, & Midrash)
Jacob's wife, Rachel was buried in Bethlehem.
(Genesis 35:19)

376
How old was Isaac when he died?
"The days of Isaac were a hundred and fourscore [180] years."
(Genesis 35:28)

377
Who were the patriarchs of Israel?
The patriarchs of Israel were Abraham, Isaac, Jacob
and the twelve sons of Jacob.
(Acts 7:8)

378
Why did God, through Jacob, set Ephraim before Manasseh?
When Jacob was old and sick,
"[Joseph] took with him
his two sons, Manasseh and Ephraim [to see Jacob].
"And Israel [Jacob] strengthened himself,
and sat upon the bed.
And Jacob said unto Joseph … thy two sons,
Ephraim and Manasseh … are mine;
as Reuben and Simeon, they shall be mine."
"And Israel [Jacob] stretched out his right hand,
and laid it upon Ephraim's head, who was the younger,
and his left had upon Manasseh's head,
guiding his hand wittingly;
for Manasseh was the first-born."
"And when Joseph saw that his father laid his right hand
upon the head of Ephraim, it displeased him:
and he held up his father's hand,
to remove it from Ephraim's head
unto Manasseh's head.
And Joseph said unto his father,
Not so, my father:
for this [Manasseh] is the first-born;
put thy right hand upon [Manasseh's] head.
And his father refused, and said,
I know it, my son, I know it:
he also shall become a people,
and he also shall be great:
but truly his younger brother shall be greater than he,
and his seed shall become a multitude of nations.
And he blessed them that day, saying,
In thee shall Israel bless, saying,
God make thee as Ephraim and as Manasseh:
and he set Ephraim before Manasseh."
(Genesis 48:1/2, 48:5, 48:14, 48:17/20)
Joshua would be a descendent of Ephraim.
(Numbers 13:8)

379
Who were the descendents from Judah to David?
Judah, Pharez, Hezron, Ram, Amminadab,
Nahshon, Salmon, Boaz, Obed, Jesse, and David.
(Genesis 46:12 & Ruth 4:18/22)

380
Who were the mothers of the children of Jacob (or Israel)?
Leah was the mother of Reuben, Simeon, Levi,
Judah, Issachar, and Zebulun.
(Genesis 35:23)
Rachel was the mother of Joseph and Benjamin.
(Genesis 35:24)
Bilhah, Rachel's handmaid, was the mother of
Dan and Naphtali.
(Genesis 35:25)
Zilpah, Leah's handmaid, was the mother of
Gad and Asher.
(Genesis 35:26)

381
In what city did God bless Jacob?
"Jacob said unto Joseph,
God Almighty appeared unto me at Luz
in the land of Canaan, and blessed me."
(Genesis 48:3)

382
Which came first the Jews or the Gentiles?
The Gentiles preceded the Jews.
The Jews are the children of Israel.
They are the descendents of Abraham
through Isaac and Jacob.
Jacob had twelve sons
and became the father of the twelve tribes of Israel.
(Genesis 49)

383

Whose sin of incest cost him his birthright?
Jacob's oldest son, Reuben.
(Genesis 49:3/4 & I Chronicles 5:1/2)

384

Why are the Jews indestructible?
Israel, the nation and the people, is a miracle of history!
Israel came into existence
in the first book of the Bible, Genesis,
and she shall realize her fulfillment
in the events of the last book of the Bible, Revelation.
God put Israel in the middle of the world,
and He is preserving her for a day
when Jerusalem shall be the capital
of the kingdom of Jesus Christ here on earth,
with the twelve tribes of Israel judging with Him.
"The scepter [or rulership] shall not depart from Judah,
nor a lawgiver from between his feet,
until Shiloh [Jesus Christ] come;
and unto him shall the gathering of the people be."
(Genesis 49:10)

385

Where was Jacob buried?
"[Jacob's] sons carried him into the land of Canaan,
and buried him in the cave of the field of Machpelah …
before Mamre."
(Genesis 50:13)

386

Moses was from what tribe?
Moses was a man of the tribe of Levi
who married a Levite woman.
(Exodus 2:1)

387
Who was Moses' sister?
Miriam was the sister of Moses and Aaron.
(Numbers 26:59)
Moses may have had another unnamed sister.
(Exodus 2:4)

388
How did God speak unto Moses?
"Moses kept the flock of Jethro his father in law, …:
and he led [them] … to the mountain of God, even Horeb.
And the angel of the Lord appeared unto [Moses]
in a flame of fire out of the midst of a bush:
and [Moses] looked, and, behold,
the bush burned with fire,
and the bush was not consumed.
And Moses said,
I will now turn aside, and see the great sight,
why the bush is not burnt.
And when the Lord saw
that [Moses] had turned aside to see,
God called unto him out of the midst of the bush,
and said,
Moses, Moses. And [Moses] said, Here am I."
(Exodus 3:1/4)

389
Why did the Lord say unto Abram,
"I am the Lord that brought thee out of Ur of the Chaldees,
to give thee this land to inherit it."?
Abram had lived in Ur of the Chaldees
with his father, Terah.
Terah had taken Abram, and Sarai and Lot
out of Ur of the Chaldees,
and they came to Haran and dwelt there until Terah died
and the Lord called Abram to leave.
(Genesis 11:31, 15:7 & Nehemiah 9:7)

390
Where did Moses go when he fled from Egypt?
"Moses fled from the face of Pharaoh,
and dwelt in the land of Midian:
and he sat down by a well."
(Exodus 2:15)

391
Who was the priest of Midian?
Reuel, whose name in Hebrew was also Jethro
(Exodus 2:18 & 3:1)

392
**Who was Moses' wife,
and how did she become his wife?**
The priest of Midian had seven daughters
who came to the well to water their father's flock.
Moses was there
and he drew water for them.
Then the priest of Midian
gave his daughter, Zipporah,
to Moses to marry.
(Exodus 2:16/21)

393
Who buried Moses and where was he buried?
The Lord buried Moses
"in a valley in the land of Moab,
over against Beth-peor."
(Deuteronomy 34:6)
Michael the archangel
may have been the Lord's agent
in the burial of Moses.
(Jude 1:9)

394
Who was Moses' son?
"Zipporah bare Moses a son,
and he called his name Gershom [meaning stranger]."
(Exodus 2:21/22)
"And Shebuel the son of Gershom,
the [grand]son of Moses,
was ruler of the treasures."
(I Chronicles 26:24)

395
What city is known as the city of David?
Bethlehem is often referred to as the city of David.
(Luke 2:4 & 2:11)
David, King of Israel, was born in Bethlehem.
Jesus the Christ was born in Bethlehem.
(Luke 2:4/7)
The prophet, Micah, prophesied
that Jesus would be born in Bethlehem.
(Micah 5:2)
Rachel died and was buried in Bethlehem.
(Genesis 35:19)
Boaz lived in Bethlehem.
Bethlehem means in Hebrew, 'House of Bread.'
Bethlehem is six miles south of Jerusalem.
Bethlehem is on a mountain 2,460 feet above sea level.
Jerusalem is also known as the City of David.
(II Samuel 5:7)

396
Where will the 144,000 sealed children of Israel be during the Great Tribulation?
They will be hidden by God
for their protection and preservation
as a remnant of Israel.
Many think they will be hidden in Petra.

397
What will be
"the battle of that great day of God Almighty?"
The battle of that great day of God Almighty
will be the battle at Armageddon.
Satan, and the Antichrist, and the false prophet
shall gather the kings of the earth and of the whole world to battle
in a place called in the Hebrew tongue Armageddon.
(Revelation 16:13/14 & 16:16)

398
When will the battle at Armageddon happen?
The battle at Armageddon will happen
at the end of the seven years of tribulation
when Jesus Christ returns from heaven to earth
to defeat the Antichrist and his armies.
This will happen when the seventh angel
pours out his vial into the air.
(Revelation 16:17)

399
How will the Antichrist and his armies
be defeated at Armageddon?
Antichrist and his armies will be defeated
by the word of Jesus Christ.
"I [John] saw heaven opened, and behold a white horse;
and he that sat upon [the horse] was called Faithful and True,
and in righteousness he doth judge and make war."
(Revelation 19:11)
"And out of his mouth goeth a sharp sword [the word of God],
that with it he should smite the nations:
and he shall rule with a rod of iron:
and treadeth the winepress
of the fierceness and wrath of Almighty God.
And he hath on his vesture and on his thigh a name written,
KING OF KINGS, AND LORD OF LORDS."
(Revelation 19:15/16)

400
What will be Satan's final rebellion
and when will Satan's final rebellion happen?
Satan's final rebellion will happen
after the Millennial rule of Jesus Christ here on earth.
"When the thousand years are expired,
Satan shall be loosed out of his prison,
And [he] shall go out to deceive the nations
which are in the four quarters of the earth,
… to gather them together to battle:
the number of whom is as the sand of the sea.'
(Revelation 20:7/8)

401
What will be the purpose of Satan's final rebellion?
The purpose of Satan's final rebellion will be to defeat Jesus Christ.
(Revelation 20:8)

402
How will Satan's armies be defeated at his final rebellion?
"[Satan's armies will go] up on the breadth of the earth,
and compass the camp of the saints about,
and the beloved city [Jerusalem]:
and fire [shall come] down from God out of heaven,
and devour them."
(Revelation 20:9)

403
Who chose to suffer affliction with the people of God?
"By faith Moses, when he was come to years,
refused to be called the son of Pharaoh's daughter;
Choosing rather to suffer affliction with the people of God,
than to enjoy the pleasures of sin for a season;
Esteeming the reproach of Christ
greater riches than the treasures in Egypt:
for he had respect unto the recompense of the reward."
(Hebrews 11:24/26)

404
Why was David "a man after [God's] own heart?"
When he heard Goliath defy God by defying Israel,
David had confidence based on his earlier experiences
that God would give him victory over Goliath.
"Then said David to [Goliath],
Thou comest to me with a sword,
and with a spear, and with a shield:
but I come to thee in the name of the Lord of hosts,
the God of the armies of Israel,
whom thou hast defied.
This day will the Lord deliver thee into mine hand;
and I will smite thee, and take thine head from thee;
and I will give the carcases of the host of the Philistines this day
unto the fowls of the air, and to the wild beasts of the earth;
that all the earth may know that there is a God in Israel."
(I Samuel 17:45/46)
This showed that David's heart for God and for Israel
was the same as God's heart for Israel.
"And when [God] had removed [Saul],
[God] raised up unto [Israel] David to be their king;
to whom also gave testimony, and said,
I have found David the son of Jesse,
a man after mine own heart,
which shall fulfill all my will."
(Acts 13:22)

405
Who was the father of Isaiah?
Amoz was the father of Isaiah.
(II Kings 19:2 & 20, 20:1, II Chronicles 26:22, 32:20 & 32,
Isaiah 1:1, 2:1, 13:1, 20:2, 37:2 & 21 & 38:1)
The Bible provides no other information about Amoz.
Amoz may have been a brother of Amaziah, king of Judah.

406
What will be the future capital city
of all the earth?
Jerusalem will be the future capital city of all the earth
during the millennial kingdom of Jesus Christ.
"Behold, the day of the Lord cometh …
And the Lord shall be king over all the earth."
(Zechariah 14:1 & 9)
Jesus Christ shall descend from heaven
to the mount of Olives
as King of kings, and Lord of lords.
(Zechariah 14:4 & Revelation 19:16)
"At that time they shall call Jerusalem the throne of the Lord;
and all the nations shall be gathered unto it,
to the name of the Lord, to Jerusalem:
neither shall they walk any more
after the imagination of their evil heart."
(Jeremiah 3:17)
After ruling on earth for a thousand years,
when all enemies have been subdued unto Jesus Christ,
then shall Jesus Christ deliver up the kingdom to God the Father,
and this earth shall be destroyed, and a new Jerusalem
will come down from heaven to a new earth.
(I Corinthians 15:24/28, II Peter 3:10 & Revelation 21:1/2)

407
A dispute about whose body caused Michael the archangel
to say to the devil, "The Lord rebuke thee?"
"Michael the archangel,
when contending with the devil
he disputed about the body of Moses,
durst not bring against [the devil] a railing accusation,
but said, The Lord rebuke thee."
(Jude 1:9)

408
Does man seek God?
"The fool hath said in his heart, There is no God.
They [all mankind] are corrupt, they have done abominable works,
there is none that doeth good.
The Lord looked down from heaven upon the children of men,
to see if there were any that did understand, and seek God.
They are all gone aside, they are all together become filthy:
there is none that doeth good, no, not one."
(Psalm 14:1/3 & 53:1/3)

409
What is called the exodus in the Bible?
The second book of the Bible is called Exodus.
It is a book about redemption.
Exodus means to depart,
and the exodus referred to in the Bible
was the departure or God's deliverance of Israel
from slavery in Egypt.
Symbolically, Egypt represented the bondage of sin.
Death of the first-born in Egypt brought about Israel's deliverance.
(Exodus 12:29)
This pointed to the death of Jesus Christ,
the first-born of God the Father,
who would deliver man from the bondage of sin
and the penalty of death.
(Romans 8:29)
"Thus the Lord saved Israel that day
out of the hand of the Egyptians;
and Israel saw the Egyptians dead upon the seashore.
And Israel saw that great work which the Lord did
upon the Egyptians: and the people feared the Lord,
and believed the Lord, and his servant Moses."
(Exodus 14:30/31)

410
What is the Passover?

The Passover is the descriptive name
of an annual eight-day Jewish observance and feast
commemorating "the sacrifice of the Lord's passover,
who passed over the houses of the children of Israel in Egypt,
when he smote the Egyptians,
and delivered [the houses of the children of Israel]."
(Exodus 12:27)
The Lord told Moses to tell the children of Israel
to kill an unblemished male lamb,
and to take of the blood,
and strike it on the two side posts
and on the upper door post of the houses.
And the Lord said,
"when I see the blood [on the door posts],
I will pass over [that house],
and the plague shall not be upon [that house]
to destroy [the first-born], when I smite the land of Egypt."
(Exodus 12:13)
"And it came to pass, that at midnight
the Lord smote all the first-born in the land of Egypt,
from the first-born of Pharaoh that sat on the throne
unto the first-born of the captive
that was in the dungeon;
and all the first-born of cattle,
[but not the first-born of the children of Israel
who had blood of the unblemished male lamb
on the door posts of their houses]."
(Exodus 12:29)
The Passover also commemorates
the birth of the nation of Israel.
Prior to the exodus from Egypt,
the children of Israel had no land
and were simply a people of the Mosaic law.

411
How does the Bible say that the Red sea was divided?
"Moses stretched out his hand over the sea
[as the Lord had told Moses to do];
and the Lord caused the sea to go back by a strong east wind
all that night, and made the sea dry land,
and the waters were divided.
And the children of Israel went into the midst of the sea
upon dry ground: and the waters were a wall unto them
on their right hand, and on their left.
And the Egyptians pursued, and went after them
to the midst of the sea, even all Pharaoh's horses,
his chariots, and his horsemen."
(Exodus 14:21/23)
"And the waters returned, and covered the chariots,
and the horsemen, and all the host of Pharaoh
that came into the sea after them [the children of Israel];
there remained not so much as one of them."
(Exodus 14:28)
"Thus the Lord saved Israel that day
out of the hand of the Egyptians;
and Israel saw the Egyptians dead upon the seashore."
(Exodus 14:30)

412
Did the Lord actually divide the waters of the Red Sea?
The Bible says that the Lord did divide the Red Sea.
"Moses stretched out his hand over the sea;
and the Lord caused the sea to go back
by a strong east wind all that night,
and made the sea dry land, and the waters were divided.
And the children of Israel
went into the midst of the sea upon dry ground:
and the waters were a wall unto them
on their right hand, and on their left."
(Exodus 14:21/22 & Hebrews 11:29)

413
What are the ten commandments of God?

"God spake all these words, saying,

1. I am the Lord thy God,
which have brought thee out of the land of Egypt,
out of the house of bondage.

2. Thou shalt have no other gods before me.
Thou shalt not make unto thee any graven images,
or any likeness of any thing that is in heaven above,
or that is in the earth beneath,
or that is in the water under the earth.
Thou shalt not bow down thyself to them, nor serve them:
for I the Lord thy God am a jealous God,
visiting the iniquity of the fathers upon the children
unto the third and fourth generations of them that hate me.
And showing mercy unto thousands of them that love me,
and keep my commandments.

3. Thou shalt not take the name of the Lord thy God in vain:
for the Lord will not hold him guiltless
that taketh his name in vain.

4. Remember the Sabbath day, to keep it holy.
Six days shalt thou labor, and do all thy work:
But the seventh day is the Sabbath of the Lord thy God:
in it thou shalt not do any work,
thou, nor thy son, nor thy daughter,
thy manservant, nor thy maidservant,
nor thy cattle, nor thy stranger that is within thy gates:
For in six days the Lord made heaven and earth,
the sea, and all that is,
and rested the seventh day:
wherefore the Lord blessed the Sabbath day,
and hallowed it.

5. Honor thy father and thy mother: that thy days may be long
upon the land which the Lord thy God giveth thee.

6. Thou shalt not kill.

7. Thou shalt not commit adultery.

8. Thou shalt not steal.

9. Thou shalt not bear false witness against thy neighbor.
10. Thou shalt not covet thy neighbor's house,
thou shalt not covet thy neighbor's wife,
nor his manservant, nor his maidservant,
nor his ox, nor his ass, nor any thing that is thy neighbor's."
(Exodus 20:1/17)

414
What in the Bible is described as the Diaspora?
Diaspora describes the dispersion of the Jews
from their homeland of Israel
from the time they were taken into Babylonian captivity
until the present time.
While many Jews have returned to the land of Israel,
Diaspora describes the Jews dwelling outside their homeland.
"And I [God] scattered them among the heathen,
and they are dispersed through the countries:
according to their way
and according to their doings I judged them."
(Ezekiel 36:19)

415
What articles were placed in the Ark of the Covenant?
The golden pot that had manna (God's Provision),
Aaron's rod that budded (God's Promise),
and the tables of the covenant (God's Precepts).
(Exodus 16:32/34, Numbers 17,
Deuteronomy 10:1/5 & Hebrews 9:3/4)

416
What did the Ark of the Covenant represent?
It represented the presence of God in ancient Israel.
It was placed in the Holy of Holies
in the tabernacle and then in Solomon's temple.
(Exodus 40 & I Kings 8)

417
Who was the prophet of Moses?
His older brother, Aaron
(Exodus 7:1 & Numbers 26:59 & I Chronicles 23:13)

418
What was Joshua's name before it was changed?
Joshua was Hoshea [Oshea]
before Moses changed his name.
He was the son of Nun Jehoshua of the tribe of Ephraim.
(Numbers 13:8 & 13:16)

419
Who slayed Korah?
Korah was slain by Jehovah with fire and earthquakes.
(Numbers 16:1/3)
Korah was a descendent of a Levitical family
with duties as doorkeepers and singers.

420
How did the Lord show the children of Israel that the tribe of Levi and the family of Aaron were chosen for the priesthood?
By making the rod of Aaron bud,
and blossom, and yield almonds.
(Numbers 17)

421
Where was Moses' sister, Miriam, buried?
"Then came the children of Israel,
even the whole congregation,
into the desert of Zin ...: and the people abode in Kadesh;
and Miriam died there, and was buried there."
(Numbers 20:1)

422
Why did God not allow Moses and Aaron
lead the children of Israel into the land
which God had given to them?

The children of Israel had contended with Moses
and complained of having no water there in the desert of Zin.
The Lord told Moses and Aaron to assemble the people
and to "speak unto the rock before their eyes;
and it shall give forth his water."
(Numbers 20:8)
Instead of speaking to the rock to sanctify or elevate the Lord,
Moses smote the rock as he had in Rephidim (Exodus 17:1/7);
this time twice in anger and disobedience.
This elevated Moses and Aaron rather than elevating the Lord.
"Because [Moses and Aaron] believed [the Lord] not,
to sanctify [the Lord] in the eyes of the children of Israel,
therefore [they were] not [allowed] to bring [the] congregation
into the land which [the Lord had] given to them."
(Numbers 20:12)

423
What is the meaning of Meribath?

Meribath means 'to strive.'
The children of Israel strove over having no water
at Rephidim in Sinai and at Kadesh in the desert of Zin.
At Rephidim, "[Moses] called the name of the place Massah,
and Meribah, because of the chiding of the children of Israel,
and because they tempted the Lord,
saying, Is the Lord among us, or not?"
(Exodus 17:7)
At Kadesh in the desert of Zin,
the place was called "the water of Meribah;
because the children of Israel strove with the Lord,
and he was sanctified [or hallowed] in them."
(Numbers 20:13)

424
What was the law about taking clothes as pledge?
Clothes taken to pledge were to be returned before sundown.
"If thou at all take thy neighbor's raiment to pledge,
thou shalt deliver it unto him by that the sun goeth down:
For that is his covering only, it is his raiment for his skin:
wherein shall he sleep?
and it shall come to pass, when he crieth unto me, that I will hear;
for I [God] am gracious."
(Exodus 22:26/27)

425
Who did the earth open and swallow before Moses?
"The earth opened her mouth, and swallowed up
[Dathan and Abiram], and their houses,
and all the men that appertained unto Korah, and their goods."
(Numbers 16:32)

426
Who was Balak?
Balak was king of Moab who hired Balaam
to curse Israel as the children of Israel took the land
which the Lord had given to them.
(Numbers 22:1/7)
"To the angel of the church in Pergamos,
… I [Jesus Christ] have a few things against thee,
because thou hast there them
that hold the doctrine of Balaam,
who taught Balak to cast a stumbling block
before the children of Israel,
to eat things sacrificed unto idols,
and to commit fornication."
(Revelation 2:14)

427
Who replaced Aaron as the high priest of the Israelites?
"Moses did as the Lord commanded:
and [Moses and Aaron and Eleazar, Aaron's son]
went up into mount Hor in the sight of all the congregation.
And Moses stripped Aaron of his [priestly] garments,
and put them upon Eleazar his son;
and Aaron died there in the top of the mount:
and Moses and Eleazar came down from the mount.
And when all the congregation saw that Aaron was dead,
they mourned for Aaron thirty days, even all the house of Israel."
(Numbers 20:26/29)

428
**What warning was given to the priests of Israel
who did not keep the covenant God gave to Levi?**
The warning was that God would take away
His covenant of peace and of an everlasting priesthood.
"If ye will not hear, and if ye will not lay it to heart,
to give glory unto my name, saith the Lord of hosts,
I will even send a curse upon you, and I will curse your blessings:
yea, I have cursed them already, because ye do not lay it to heart."
(Numbers 25:12 & Malachi 2:2)

429
Who were Moses' parents?
Amram was Moses' father,
and Jochebed was Moses' mother.
(Numbers 26:59)

430
Where did God speak to Moses?
"The Lord spake unto Moses in the plains of Moab
by Jordan near Jericho."
(Numbers 33:50 & 35:1)

431
What in the Bible is to be the Year of Jubilee?
The Year of Jubilee was to be a year of release and liberty
to be observed in the land of Israel.
"Thou shalt number seven sabbaths of years unto thee,
seven times seven years;
and the space of the seven sabbaths of years
shall be unto thee forty and nine years.
Then shalt thou cause the trumpet of the jubilee to sound
on the tenth day of the seventh month, in the day of atonement
shall ye make the trumpet sound throughout all your land.
And ye shall hallow the fiftieth year, and proclaim liberty
throughout all the land unto all the inhabitants thereof:
it shall be a jubilee unto you;
and ye shall return every man unto his possession,
and ye shall return every man unto his family.
A jubilee shall that fiftieth year be unto you:
ye shall not sow,
neither reap that which growth of itself in it,
nor gather the grapes in it of thy vine undressed."
(Leviticus 25:8/11)
(See also the remainder of Leviticus 25,
Leviticus 27 & Numbers 36:4)

432
What are the boundaries of the land promised to Israel?
"From the wilderness [Negev in the south]
[to] Lebanon [in the north]
even unto the great river,
the river Euphrates [to the east],
all the land of the Hittites,
and unto the Great Sea
toward the going down of the sun
[or to the west],
shall be your coast."
(Joshua 1:4)

433
Who wrote the first five books of the Bible?
Moses wrote the first five books
with the exception of Deuteronomy 34,
which tells about the death and burial of Moses
and his succession by Joshua.
(Joshua 1:7/8 & John 1:17)

434
Was the Red sea the only body of water divided?
No, the waters of the river Jordan were also divided.
"And it came to pass, when the people [the Israelites]
removed from their tents, to pass over Jordan,
and the priests bearing the ark of the covenant before the people;
And as they that bare the ark were come unto Jordan,
and the feet of the priests that bare the ark
were dipped in the brim of the water,
[for Jordan overfloweth all his banks all the time of the harvest,]
That the waters which came down from above stood and rose up
upon a heap very far from the city Adam, that is beside Zaretan:
and those [waters] that came down toward the sea of the plain,
even the Salt Sea, failed, and were cut off:
and the people passed over right against Jericho.
And the priests that bare the ark of the covenant of the Lord
stood firm on dry ground in the midst of Jordan,
and all the Israelites passed over on dry ground,
until all the people were passed clean over Jordan."
(Joshua 3:14/17)

435
When the Israelites passed over the river Jordan where did they set up their encampment?
The Israelites set up their encampment in Gilgal.
"And the people came up out of Jordan
on the tenth day of the first month,
and encamped in Gilgal, in the east border of Jericho."
(Joshua 4:19)

436

**What city's wall fell down flat
at the blowing of trumpets
and at the shouting of the children of Israel?**
The wall fell around the city of Jericho.
(Joshua 6:20)

437

On what occasion did the sun stand still?
"Spake Joshua to the Lord
in the day when the Lord delivered up the Amorites
before the children of Israel, and he [Joshua] said,
Sun, stand thou still upon Gibeon;
and thou, Moon, in the valley of Ajalon.
And the sun stood still, and the moon stayed,
until the people had avenged themselves upon their enemies.
… So the sun stood still in the midst of heaven,
and hasted not to go down about a whole day.
And there was no day like that before it or after it,
that the Lord hearkened unto the voice of a man:
for the Lord fought for Israel."
(Joshua 10:12/14)

438

**How old was Joshua when he died,
and where was he buried?**
Joshua died when he was 110 years old.
He was buried in Timnath-serah
(Joshua 24:29/30)

439

Who was Joshua's father?
The father of Joshua was Nun.
(Exodus 33:11 & Numbers 11:28, 14:6, 30 & 38, 26:65, 27:18,
32:12 & 28, 34:17, Deuteronomy 1:38, 31:23, & 34:9,
Joshua 1:1, 2:1 & 23, 6:6, 14:1, 17:4, 19:49 & 51,
21:1, 24:29, Judges 2:8 & I Kings 16:34)

440
Who was Caleb's father?
The father of Caleb was Jephunneh.
(Numbers 13:6, 14:6, 30 & 38, 26:65, 32:12, 34:19,
Deuteronomy 1:35, Joshua 14:6, 13 & 14, 15:13 & 21:12,
I Chronicles 4:15 & 6:56)

441
After the children of Israel took the promised land, where did they set up the tabernacle?
The tabernacle was set up at Shiloh in the promised land.
(Joshua 18:1)

442
Where were the bones of Joseph buried?
Joseph's bones were buried at Shechem.
(Joshua 24:32)

443
What did the children of Israel do wrong after Joshua died?
"They forsook the Lord God of their fathers,
which brought them out of the land of Egypt,
and followed other gods,
of the gods of the people that were round about them,
and bowed themselves unto them,
and provoked the Lord to anger.
And they forsook the Lord, and served Baal and Ashtaroth."
(Judges 2:8 & 2:12/13)
Ashtaroth is plural of Ashtoreth.

444
Who were the judges of Israel?
The judges of Israel were:
Otheniel (3:9), Ehud (3:15), Shamgar (3:31), Deborah (4:4),
Gideon 6:7), Tola (10:1), Jair (10:3), Jephthah (10:10),
Ibzan (12:8), Elon (12:11), Abdon (12:13), and Samson (13:2).
(The Book of Judges)

445
Who was Gideon?
Gideon was a prophet
sent unto the children of Israel by the Lord
to deliver them from bondage to the Midianites.
(Judges 6:1/7)
Even though Gideon was the least in his father's house,
the angel of the Lord called Gideon a mighty man of valour.
(Judges 6:12)

446
Who was the father of Samson?
Manoah, a Danite, was Samson's father.
(Judges 13:2)

447
What is the primary theme of the Books of Samuel?
The establishment of the throne
of the kingdom of Israel.
Prayer and the rise of the office of prophet
are also themes of these books.

448
Who was described as Hannah's adversary?
Peninnah, the other wife of Elkanah,
provoked Hannah because
"Peninnah had children,
but Hannah had no children."
(I Samuel 1:1/6)

449
Who were Samuel's parents?
Elkanah was Samuel's father,
and Hannah was Samuel's mother.
(I Samuel 1:19/20)

450

Why was Samuel taken to the temple at Shiloh and not to Jerusalem?

The temple at Jerusalem was not built until after Samuel died.
The tabernacle was at Shiloh
and was sometimes called the temple.
(I Samuel 1:24)
King Solomon built the first temple at Jerusalem.
Samuel died while David was king.

451

Did Israel always possess the ark of the covenant?

When Israel went out against the Philistines to battle,
the people said,
"Let us fetch the ark of the covenant of the Lord
out of Shiloh unto us, that when it cometh among us,
it may save us out of the hand of our enemies."
But the Philistines defeated Israel
and took the ark of God.
(I Samuel 4:1/11)

452

How was the ark returned from the Philistines to Israel?

Possessing the ark of God
brought God's wrath upon the Philistines,
so they returned the ark to Israel
by placing the ark on a cart hitched to two cows,
and the two cows "took the straight way
to the way of Beth-shemesh,"
and the ark was placed in the house of Abinadab
where it stayed for twenty years.
(I Samuel 5:1 / 7:2)

453

What was a prophet in Israel called other than a prophet?

A prophet was called a Seer.
(I Samuel 9:9)

454
What musical instrument did David play?
David played the harp.
(I Samuel 16:23)

455
Who was Goliath?
"There went out [to battle against Israel]
a champion of the camp of the Philistines,
named Goliath, of Gath,
whose height was six cubits and a span."
(I Samuel 17:1 & 4)

456
Where did David slay Goliath?
David slew Goliath in the valley of Elah,
which was part of Judah.
(I Samuel 17:1/2 & 21:9)

457
What does the Bible say is better than sacrifice?
The world says it is easier to ask for forgiveness
than to obtain permission,
but "Samuel said,
Hath the Lord as great delight
in burnt offerings and sacrifices,
as in obeying the voice of the Lord?
Behold, to obey is better than sacrifice,
and to hearken [or obey is better] than the fat of rams."
(I Samuel 15:22)

458
What is the last mention of Jesse in the Bible?
David sent his father, Jesse, and his mother
to Moab for their safety.
(I Samuel 22:3/4)
There is no subsequent mention of Jesse in the Bible.

459

**Who was the churlish man of the house of Caleb
who refused to help David?**
Nabal "was churlish and evil in his doings."
(I Samuel 25:3)
He refused to help David.
(I Samuel 25:10/11)

460

Who was the wife of Nabal who became the wife of David?
Abigail was the wife of Nabal.
(I Samuel 25:3)
After Nabal was dead,
David took Abigail to be his wife.
(I Samuel 25:39/42)

461

**Who was struck down and died
for reaching out and taking hold of the ark of God?**
"When they came to Nachon's threshing floor,
Uzzah put forth his hand to the ark of God,
and took hold of it;
for the oxen shook it.
And the anger of the Lord was kindled against Uzzah;
and God smote him there for his error;
and there he died by the ark of God."
(II Samuel 6:6/7)

462

Who were the sons of Jesse?
Jesse had eight sons.
Eliab, Abinadab, Shammah, Nethaneel, Radai, Ozem,
One Unnamed & David
(I Samuel 16:6/13 & I Chronicles 2:14/15)

463
Who were the first three men to be king of all Israel?
Saul was the first man to be king of Israel.
(I Samuel 11:15)
David succeeded Saul as king of Israel.
(II Samuel 2:, 5:3 & 12:7)
And Solomon, David's son,
succeeded David as king of Israel.
(I Kings 1:39)

464
Why did David have Uriah killed?
David had seen Uriah's wife, Bathsheba
"washing herself;
and [she] was very beautiful to look upon."
(II Samuel 11:3)
David "enquired after [Bathsheba], ...,
and sent messengers, and took her;
and she came in unto him,
and he lay with her, ... and [she] conceived."
(II Samuel 11:3/5)
Then after David tried unsuccessfully to hide his sin
(II Samuel 11:6/13)
he told Joab,
who headed Israel's battle against Ammon,
to "Set ye Uriah in the forefront of the hottest battle,
and retire ye from him,
that he may be smitten, and die."
(II Samuel 11:1 &15)

465
Who were the father and mother of Solomon?
David was Solomon's father,
and Bathsheba was Solomon's mother.
(II Samuel 12:24 & Matthew 1:6)

466
Whose wife was Bathsheba before she was David's wife?
Bathsheba was the wife of Uriah [Urias]
before David took her to wife.
(II Samuel 12:24 & Matthew 1:6)

467
Who were the father and mother of David?
Jesse was David's father,
and David's mother is not named in the Bible.
(I Samuel 22:3 & Matthew 1:6)
The Talmud identifies David's mother as Nitzevet,
daughter of Adael.

468
What was the shekinah glory?
The shekinah glory was the visible presence of God
dwelling with His people, the children of Israel.
After the ark of God was brought into the temple,
and "when the priests were come out of the holy place,
… the glory of the Lord … filled the house of the Lord."
(I Kings 8:10/11)

469
What happened to Israel after king Solomon died?
Israel was divided into two kingdoms,
one consisting of the ten northern tribes
which kept the name of Israel,
and another consisting of the two southern tribes
of Judah and Benjamin
which took the name of Judah.
Jeroboam became king of Israel,
and Rehoboam became king of Judah.
(I Kings 11)

470

What were the capital cities of the ten northern tribes of Israel?

Jeroboam, king of Israel, dwelt in Shechem.
Later king Baasha made Tirzah the capital city of Israel.
Then, Omri became king of Israel
and built a city on the hill of Samaria of Shemer.
Samaria then became the capital city of Israel.
(I Kings 12:25, 15:33 & 16:24)

471

Who made Israel to sin?

Jeroboam made Israel to sin.
(I Kings 14:16 & 15:30)

472

How did Jeroboam make Israel to sin?

Jeroboam was king of the ten northern tribes of Israel.
He did not want the "people [to] go up to do sacrifice
in the house of the Lord at Jerusalem
[because] the heart of [the] people [would] turn again
unto their lord, even unto Rehoboam king of Judah,
and they [would] kill [Jeroboam]."
(I Kings 12:27)
"Whereupon [Jeroboam] ... made two calves of gold,
and said unto [the people],
It is too much for you to go up to Jerusalem:
behold thy gods, O Israel,
which brought thee up out of the land of Egypt.
And he set the one in Bethel, and the other put he in Dan.
And this thing became a sin:
for the people went to worship before [them].
And [Jeroboam] made a house of high places,
and made priests of the lowest of the people,
which were not of the sons of Levi."
(I Kings 12:28/31, See also 12:32/33)

473
How many times does the Bible say
that Jeroboam made Israel to sin?
The Bible says twenty times that Jeroboam made Israel to sin.
(I Kings 14:16, 15:30 & 34, 16:2 & 26, 21:22, 22:52,
II Kings 3:3, 10:29 & 31, 13:2, 6 & 11,
14:24, 15:9, 18, 24 & 28, 17:21 & 23:15)

474
Who was the father of Jeroboam?
Nebat was the father of Jeroboam, king of Israel.
(I Kings 11:26, 12:2 & 15, 15:1, 16:3, 26 & 31, 21:22, 22:52,
II Kings 3:3, 9:9, 10:29, 13:2 & 11, 14:24, 15:9, 18, 24, & 28,
17:21, 23:15, II Chronicles 9:29, 10:2 & 15 & 13:6)

475
What happened to the kingdom of Judah?
"Nebuchadnezzar king of Babylon came,
he, and all his host, against Jerusalem,
and the city was besieged …
and all the men of might …
the king of Babylon brought captive to Babylon."
(II Kings 24:10 & 16)
This event known as the Babylonian Captivity
took place in 605 B.C. through 586 B.C.

476
Who was Jezebel in the Bible?
Jezebel was the wife of Ahab, king of Israel,
who served Baal and worshiped him.
She was "the daughter of Ethbaal
king of the Zidonians."
(I Kings 16:31)

477
**How did the Lord use and bless
the widow woman of Zarephath?**
"The word of the Lord came unto [Elijah], saying,
Arise, get thee to Zarephath, which belongeth to Zidon,
and dwell there:
behold, I have commanded a widow woman there to sustain thee."
(I Kings 17:8/9)
The widow woman fed Elijah with the last handful of meal and oil
that she had for herself and her son.
And the Lord blessed her
that "the barrel of meal wasted not, neither did the cruse of oil fail,
according to the word of the Lord, which he spake by Elijah."
(I Kings 17:13/16)

478
What happened later to the widow woman's son?
Later the widow woman's son died,
and the Lord revived him in answer to Elijah's prayer.
(I Kings 17:17/24)

479
Who was Obadiah?
Obadiah was the governor of the house of Ahab,
king of Israel in Samaria.
(I Kings 18:3)

480
Who hid a hundred prophets of the Lord from Jezebel?
"When Jezebel cut off the prophets of the Lord,
… Obadiah took an hundred prophets,
and hid them by fifty in a cave,
and fed them with bread and water."
(I Kings 18:4)

481
Why did Elijah flee from Jezebel?
Jezebel threatened to kill Elijah.
After Elijah slayed all the prophets of Baal,
"Jezebel sent a messenger unto Elijah, saying,
So let the gods do to me, and more also,
if I make not thy life as the life of one of them
[the prophets of Baal]
by tomorrow about this time."
(I Kings 19:2)

482
Who claimed to be the only one left
of the children of Israel who had not forsaken
the covenant of God?
"[Elijah] said,
I have been jealous for the Lord God of hosts:
because the children of Israel have forsaken thy covenant,
thrown down thine altars,
and slain thy prophets with the sword;
and I, even I only, am left;
and they seek my life, to take it away."
(I Kings 19:14)

483
What was God's response to Elijah's claim
that he was the only one left of the children of Israel
who had not forsaken God's covenant?
The Lord God responded to Elijah, saying,
"I have left me seven thousand in Israel,
all the knees which have not bowed unto Baal,
and every mouth which hath not kissed him."
(I Kings 19:18)

484
Who did Jezebel have killed to obtain his vineyard for Ahab?
"Ahab spake unto Naboth, saying,
Give me thy vineyard.
And Naboth said to Ahab, The Lord forbid it me,
that I should give the inheritance of my fathers unto thee."
(I Kings 21:2/3)
So Jezebel had two men bear false witness against Naboth,
and they stoned Naboth to death.
(I Kings 21:8/13)

485
What happened to Jezebel?
Jezebel was thrown down from the wall of Jezreel.
Jehu trode her under foot of the horses,
and the dogs ate her flesh.
(I Kings 21:23 & II Kings 9:10 & 9:33/36)

486
How does the Bible describe the wickedness of Ahab?
"There was none like unto Ahab,
which did sell himself to work wickedness
in the sight of the Lord,
whom Jezebel his wife stirred up."
(I Kings 21:25)

487
How was Elijah taken up into heaven?
As Elijah and Elisha went toward Jordan,
"it came to pass, … that, behold,
there appeared a chariot of fire, and horses of fire,
and parted them both asunder;
and Elijah went up by a whirlwind into heaven."
(II Kings 2:6 & 11)

488
Who, other than Enoch, never died?
"By faith Enoch was translated that he should not see death;
… for before his translation he had this testimony,
that he pleased God."
(Hebrews 11:5)
"And it came to pass, as [Elijah and Elisha]
still went on, and talked, that,
behold, there appeared a chariot of fire, and horses of fire,
and parted them both asunder;
and Elijah went up by a whirlwind into heaven."
(II Kings 2:11)

489
On what occasion in the Bible did iron swim?
Elisha and his students, the sons of the prophets,
went unto Jordan to build a place to dwell and to study.
"As one [of the sons of the prophets] was felling a [tree],
the axe head fell into the water [of the Jordan river]:
and he cried [to Elisha], and said, Alas, master!
for it was borrowed.
And [Elisha] said, Where fell it? And he showed [Elisha] the place.
And [Elisha] cut down a stick,
and cast it in [the water where the axe head fell];
and the iron did swim. Therefore said [Elisha],
Take it up to thee. And he put out his hand and took it."
(II Kings 6:1/7)

490
Who was king of Assyria
when Israel was taken into captivity?
Shalmaneser was king of Assyria
when Israel was taken into Assyrian captivity.
(II Kings 18:9)

491
Who was Sennacherib
and what happened when he invaded Jerusalem?
Sennacherib was king of Assyria when Assyria invaded Judah.
"Assyria [came] up against all the fenced cities of Judah,
and took them."
(II Kings 18:13)
Then Sennacherib's army came up to Jerusalem,
and Rab-shakeh, a leader of Assyria's army,
tried to intimidate the people of Jerusalem
to get them to surrender to Sennacherib.
(II Kings 18: 28/32)
Hezekiah, king of Judah prayed to the Lord.
"And it came to pass that night,
that the angel of the Lord went out,
and smote in the camp of the Assyrians
a hundred four-score and five thousand [185,000]:
and when [the people of Jerusalem] arose in the morning,
behold, they [the 185,000] were all dead corpses."
(II Kings 19:35)

492
What happened to the kingdom of Israel?
"In the days of Pekah king of Israel
came Tiglathpileser king of Assyria,
and took Ijon, and Abelbethmaachah,
and Janoah, and Kedesh, and Hazor,
and Gilead, and Galilee,
and all the land of Naphtali,
and carried them captive to Assyria."
(II Kings 15:29)
This event known as
the Assyrian Exile of the Israelites
happened in 735 B.C.

493
**Who was the son of Ahaziah
who was rescued from his grandmother's attempt
to kill all of Ahaziah's successors?**
Joash, a son of Ahaziah,
was rescued by Ahaziah's sister, Jehosheba,
and Joash was later crowned as king of Judah
by the priest, Jehoiada.
Joash's grandmother was Athaliah.
(II Kings 11:1/12)
"The … acts of Joash, … are … written
in the book of the chronicles of the kings of Judah."
(II Kings 12:19)
"And Joash did that which was right
in the sight of the Lord
all the days of Jehoiada the priest."
(II Chronicles 24:2)

494
Whose sin made him the troubler of Israel?
Achar was the troubler of Israel.
(I Chronicles 2:7 & Joshua 7)

495
Who was Iddo?
Iddo was a prophet, and a ruler of Manasseh.
(II Chronicles 9:29, 12:15 & 13:22, Zechariah 1:1 & 7,
& I Chronicles 27:16 & 21)
He was the father or grandfather of Zechariah,
and a leader in Judah's return
from the Babylonian captivity.
(Ezra 5:1 & 6:14 & Zechariah 1:1 & 7 & 8:17)

496

Who does the Bible say had more riches and wisdom than all the kings of the earth?
"King Solomon passed all the kings of the earth
in riches and wisdom."
(II Chronicles 9:22)

497

Who were Baal and Ashtoreth?
Baal and Ashtoreth represent false gods and goddesses
of the people in and around the land of Canaan.
Baal (also Baalim) is a Semitic title of various false gods.
Ashtoreth (also Astarte and Ashtoret)
was a false goddess of fertility, sexuality and war.
Baal is associated with high places,
and Ashtoreth is associated with groves.
When Asa succeeded Abijah as king over Judah,
"he took away the altars of the strange gods,
and the high places, and brake down the images,
and cut down the groves:
And commanded Judah
to seek the Lord God of their fathers,
and to do the law and the commandments."
(II Chronicles 14:3/4)

498

Whose mother counseled him to do wickedly?
"[Ahaziah] reigned one year in Jerusalem.
His mother's name ... was Athaliah,
the daughter of Omri.
He also walked in the ways of the house of Ahab:
for his mother was his counsellor to do wickedly."
(II Chronicles 22:2/3)

499
How did Esther become queen to Ahasuerus, king of Persia?
King Ahasuerus had put aside or divorced queen Vashti
for refusing to obey his commands,
and a beauty contest of fair young virgins was conducted
with king Ahasuerus choosing Esther to become queen.
(Esther 1:10 / 2:9)

500
Who was the father of Mordecai?
Jair, a judge of Israel,
was the father of Mordecai.
Mordecai was of the tribe of Benjamin.
(Esther 2:5)

501
What was Esther's Hebrew name?
Esther's Hebrew name was Hadassah.
She was Mordecai's cousin, his uncle's daughter.
Her parents had died, and Mordecai took her as his daughter.
(Esther 2:7)
"Esther had not showed her people nor her kindred
[that she was a Jew]:
for Mordecai had charged her
that she should not show it."
(Esther 2:10)

502
What was Shushan?
Shushan [Susa] was the ancient capital of Elam,
which is the southwestern portion of modern Iran.
Most of the events in the Book of Esther
took place in Shushan.
(Esther 1:2)

503

What is the Jewish celebration of Purim?
Purim is the name of an annual two-day Jewish celebration
commemorating deliverance from a plot by Haman
to annihilate the Jews.
The story is recorded in the Book of Esther.
(Esther 9:20/32)
'Purim' means 'lots'.
Haman, the second in command of Persia,
cast lots to determine
the day when the Jews would be killed.
(Esther 3:6/7)

504

What was Haman's plot?
Haman was an enemy of the Jews, and he plotted to kill them
throughout the provinces of Ahasuerus' kingdom.
(Esther 3:8/10)

505

Who claimed her husband by sleeping at his feet?
Ruth slept at the feet of Boaz
and asked him to marry her.
"When Boaz had eaten and drunk, and his heart was merry,
he went to lie down at the end of the heap of corn:
and [Ruth] came softly, and uncovered his feet, and laid her down.
And it came to pass at midnight, that [Boaz] was afraid,
and turned himself:
and, behold, a woman lay at his feet.
And he said, Who art thou?
And she answered, I am Ruth thine handmaid:
spread therefore thy skirt over thine handmaid;
for thou art a near kinsman."
(Ruth 3:7/9)
For a woman to ask a man to spread his skirt over her
was to ask him to take her as his wife.
This was consistent with Jewish tradition and was not improper.

506
Who was Naomi?
Naomi was the wife of Elimelech and the mother-in-law of Ruth.
(Ruth 1:2/4)

507
Who was Naomi's daughter-in-law
who returned to her mother's house?
Orpah was Naomi's daughter-in-law
who returned to her mother's house.
(Ruth 1:8 & 14)

508
What transition did Isaiah foresee and prophesy?
Isaiah prophesied a transition to the times of the Gentiles.
The times of the Gentiles began in 605 B.C.
with the Babylonian captivity of Judah.
It was preceded by the Assyrian conquest
of the ten northern tribes of Israel in 721 B. C.

509
How did Isaiah prophesy the birth of Jesus
as the Prince of Peace?
"Unto us a child is born, unto us a son is given:
and the government shall be upon his shoulder:
and his name shall be called Wonderful, Counselor,
The mighty God, The everlasting Father,
The Prince of Peace.
Of the increase of his government and
peace there shall be no end,
upon the throne of David, and upon his kingdom, to order it,
and to establish it with judgment and with justice
from henceforth even for ever.
The zeal of the Lord of hosts will perform this."
(Isaiah 9:6/7)

510
**What sign did Isaiah tell king Ahaz
that God would give to the house of David?**
"The Lord himself shall give you a sign;
Behold, a virgin shall conceive, and bear a son,
and shall call his name Immanuel."
(Isaiah 7:14)
"[But] before the child shall know to refuse the evil,
and choose the good, the land that thou abhorrest
shall be forsaken of both her kings."
(Isaiah 7:16)

511
Was Satan cast out of heaven in Genesis?
Satan was cast out of the third heaven (II Corinthians 12:2),
to the second heaven and to earth.
This is based in part on scriptures from Isaiah and Revelation.
"How art thou fallen from heaven, O Lucifer,
son of the morning!
how art thou cut down to the ground,
which did weaken the nations!"
(Isaiah 14:12)
"And the [great red dragon's] tail
drew the third part of the stars [or angels] of heaven;
and did cast them to the earth:
and the dragon stood before the woman [Israel]
which was ready to be delivered,
for to devour her child as soon as it was born."
(Revelation 12:3/4)
The following scriptures shows that Satan had been cast down.
"There was a day when the sons of God
[probably meaning the sons of Shem]
came to present themselves before the Lord,
and Satan came also among them.
And the Lord said unto Satan, Whence cometh thou?
Then Satan answered the Lord, and said,
From going to and fro in the earth,

and walking up and down in it."
All this probably happened on earth.
(Job 1:6/7)
The following scripture tells us that Satan has access now
to appear before the throne of God in heaven.
"And I [John] heard a loud voice saying in heaven,
Now is come salvation, and strength,
and the kingdom of our God, and the power of his Christ:
for the accuser of the brethren [believers] is cast down,
which accused them before our God day and night."
This was prophesy that will happen in the future.
(Revelation 12:10)
Satan loses access
to appear before the throne of God in heaven
at the mid-point of the Tribulation period
when he is cast down and indwells the wounded Antichrist.
(Revelation 12:9 & 13:3)

512
What happened to Isaiah?
The Bible does not record what happened to Isaiah,
but it is reported in Lives of the Prophets
that king Manasseh had Isaiah sawn in two
and buried in the area of the Pool of Siloam.

513
What are the seven spirits of the Lord?
"The spirit of wisdom and understanding,
the spirit of counsel and might,
the spirit of knowledge and of the fear of the Lord."
(Isaiah 11:2)
And the spirit of righteousness.
(Isaiah 11:3/4)

514
Which verses of the Bible describe the attitude of Satan?
"[Satan] hath said in [his] heart,
I will ascend into heaven,
I will exalt my throne above the stars of God:
I will sit also upon the mount of the congregation,
in the sides of the north:
I will ascend above the heights of the clouds;
I will be like the most High."
(Isaiah 14:13/14)

515
How will the seven remaining years that God determined upon the children of Israel and upon Jerusalem be fulfilled?
There will be a seven year period of tribulation
known as the time of Jacob's trouble
that will be fulfilled in the future.
"Alas," Jeremiah prophesied,
"for that day [a seven year period] is great,
so that none is like it:
it is even the time of Jacob's trouble,
but he [Israel] shall be saved out of it."
(Jeremiah 30:7)

516
What is unique about geographic directions in the Bible?
Geographic directions in the Bible are relative to Jerusalem.
Jerusalem is at the center of the earth.
"Thus saith the Lord God;
This is Jerusalem: I have set it in the midst [or middle]
of the nations and countries that are round about her."
(Ezekiel 5:5)

517
How and why did God depart from the temple?
God departed the temple reluctantly
because the children of Israel went
"a whoring after their idols."
(Ezekiel 6:9 & 10:1/22)

518
**Whom did the Lord make a watchman
unto the house of Israel?**
Ezekiel was made a watchman unto Israel.
"O son of man [Ezekiel],
I [the Lord] have set thee a watchman
unto the house of Israel;
therefore thou shalt hear the word at my mouth,
and warn them [of the house of Israel] from me."
(Ezekiel 33:7)

519
**Who was king of the Medes and who was king of Persia
when Babylon was defeated?**
Darius was king of the Medes, and Cyrus was king of Persia
when Babylon was defeated.
(Daniel 9:1)

520
**Who was king of Babylon
when Babylon was defeated by the Medes and Persians?**
Belshazzar was king of Babylon
when Babylon was defeated by the Medes and Persians.
(Daniel 5:28/30)

521

Who was king of Babylon when Judah was taken captive?
Nebuchadnezzar was king of Babylon
when Judah was taken into Babylonian captivity.
(Daniel 1:1)

522

**How many of the 490 years that God determined upon
the children of Israel and upon Jerusalem have been fulfilled?**
Of the 490 years that God determined
upon the children of Israel and upon Jerusalem,
483 years (49 years + 434 years) have been fulfilled,
and seven years are yet to be fulfilled in the future.
"Know therefore and understand,
that from the going forth of the commandment
[of Darius in 445 B.C.]
to restore and to build Jerusalem unto Messiah the Prince
shall be seven weeks [49 years]:"
… the street shall be built again, and the wall,
even in troublous times [finished in 397 B.C.]."
(Daniel 9:25, Nehemiah 2:1)
"[Then] after threescore and two weeks [434 years]
shall Messiah [the Prince] be cut off [crucified in A.D. 37]."
(Daniel 9:25/26)
Clocking of the 490 years stopped when
Jesus Christ was crucified.

523

**For what purposes were the seventy weeks
determined upon the children of Israel and upon Jerusalem?**
"Seventy weeks [were] determined upon [Daniel's] people
and upon thy holy city [of Jerusalem]
to finish the transgression, and to make an end of sins,
and to make reconciliation for iniquity,
and to bring in everlasting righteousness,
and to seal up the vision and prophecy,
and to anoint the most Holy."
(Daniel 9:24)

524

**How many years did God determine
upon the children of Israel
and upon the holy city of Jerusalem?**
Gabriel appeared to Daniel and informed him that
"Seventy weeks [70 times 7 + 490 years]
are determined upon thy people and upon thy holy city."
(Daniel 9:20/24)

525

**Who was the king who commanded
that Daniel be cast into the den of lions?**
Darius was king of the Medes and Persians.
"[He] commanded, and they brought Daniel,
and cast him into the den of lions."
(Daniel 6:16)

526

What have been the four world powers of history?
Babylon, Medo-Persia, Greece and Rome
(See Daniel 2:28/45)

527

What was the handwriting on the wall?
Mene, Mene, Tekel, Upharsin
Numbered, Numbered, Weighted and Divided
(Daniel 5:25)

528

**In the Babylonian captivity what new names were given
to Daniel, Hananiah, Mishael, and Azariah?**
"The prince of the eunuchs [in Babylon] gave names:
for he gave unto Daniel the name of Belteshazzar;
and [he gave] to Hananiah [the name] of Shadrach;
and [he gave] to Mishael [the name] of Meshach;
and [he gave] to Azariah [the name] of Abednego."
(Daniel 1:6/7)

529

**How does the Bible describe
the image Nebuchadnezzar saw in his first dream?**
"Thy dream, and the visions of thy head upon thy bed,
are these: … Thou, O king, sawest, and behold a great image.
This great image, whose brightness was excellent,
stood before thee; and the form thereof was terrible.
This image's head was of fine gold,
his breast and his arms of silver,
his belly and his thighs of brass, his legs of iron,
[and] his feet part of iron and part of clay."
(Daniel 2:26/33)

530

**What was represented by the image
Nebuchadnezzar saw in his first dream?**
God in heaven revealed and made known
to king Nebuchadnezzar "what shall be in the latter days."
(Daniel 2:28)
The image was a revelation of dominant world powers.
The head of fine gold represented king Nebuchadnezzar
and the Babylonian kingdom.
The breast and arms of silver represented
the Medo-Persian kingdom which succeeded Babylonia.
The belly and thighs of brass represented
the kingdom of Greece under king Alexander the Great.
The legs of iron represented the Roman Empire.
And the feet part of iron and part of clay represented
the yet future revival of the Roman Empire
as a confederation of nations to be lead by the Antichrist.
(Daniel 2:37/43)

531

What did Shadrach, Meshach, and Abednego refuse to do?
They refused to "fall down and worship
the image [of Nebuchadnezzar]."
(Daniel 3:15/18)

532
**What was the size of the golden image
of Nebuchadnezzar?**
(Sixty cubits by six cubits.)

533
Who was the woman named Gomer?
Gomer became the promiscuous wife of the prophet Hosea.
(Hosea 1:3)
Gomer represents Israel turning aside from God to idolatry.
Hosea represents God's love and desire
for Israel to return to Him.
(Hosea 14)

534
Who was the father of Hosea's wife, Gomer?
The father of Gomer, Hosea's wife, was Diblaim.
(Hosea 1:3)

535
Who was the first son of Hosea and Gomer?
Jezreel was the name of Hosea and Gomer's first son.
(Hosea 1:3/4)

536
Who was the mother of Lo-ruhamah and Lo-ammi?
Gomer, Hosea's wife,
was the mother of Lo-ruhamah and Lo-ammi.
(Hosea 1:6/9)
Lo-ruhamah means no mercy. Lo-ammi means not my people.

537
Which book of the Bible is about the Great Day of the Lord?
The Book of Joel is about the Great Day of the Lord.
(See also Zephaniah)

538
Was Amos a prophet's son?
"Amos said to Amaziah, I was no prophet,
neither was I a prophet's son;
but I was a herdman, and a gatherer of sycamore fruit:
And the Lord took me …
and said unto me,
Go, prophesy unto my people Israel."
(Amos 7:14/15)

539
Who was Jonah's father and what is
the meaning of his name?
"Jonah [was] the son of Amittai, whose name means 'Truth.'
(Jonah 1:1)

540
Why did the Lord send Jonah to Nineveh?
The Lord said to Jonah, "Arise, go to Nineveh,
that great city, and cry against it;
for their wickedness is come up before me."
(Jonah 1:1/2)

541
What happened to Jonah
when he ran from the presence of the Lord?
Jonah took a ship going to Tarshish
in the opposite direction of Nineveh,
but the Lord sent out a great wind into the sea,
and the mariners cast Jonah into the sea.
The Lord had prepared a great fish to swallow up Jonah,
and Jonah was in the belly of the fish three days and three nights.
(Jonah 1:3/17)

542

What river was parted and on what occasions?
The Jordan River was parted on several occasions.
First, for the children of Israel to cross over
and enter the land of Canaan.
"It came to pass, when the people removed from their tents,
to pass over Jordan,
and the priests bearing the ark of the covenant before the people;
And as they that bare the ark were come unto Jordan,
and the feet of the priests that bare the ark
were dipped in the brim of the water,
[for Jordan overfloweth all his banks all the time of harvest],
That the waters which came down from above
stood and rose up a heap very far from the city Adam,
that is beside Zaretan:
and those that came down toward the sea of the plain,
even the Salt Sea, failed, and were cut off:
and the people passed over right against Jericho.
And the priests that bare the ark of the covenant of the Lord
stood firm on dry ground in the midst of Jordan,
and all the Israelites passed over on dry ground,
until all the people were passed clean over Jordan."
(Joshua 3:14/17)
And for Elijah and Elisha to cross as they went to Jordan.
"Elijah took his mantle, and wrapped it together,
and smote the waters,
and they were divided hither and thither,
so that they two went over on dry ground."
(II Kings 2:8)

543

**How many times does the Song of Moses
appear in the Bible?**
The Song of Moses is a Song of Triumph.
It appears five times in the Bible.
(Exodus 15:1/19, Deuteronomy 32:1/43,
Psalm 118, Isaiah 12, & Revelation 15)

544
What is the fruit of the righteous?
"The fruit of the righteous is a tree of life;
and he that winneth souls is wise."
(Proverbs 11:30)

545
How many people named Zechariah or Zacharias
are mentioned in the Bible?
Three prominent people in the Bible
are named Zechariah or Zacharias.
One was a priest who was the father of John the Baptist
and husband of Elisabeth, a cousin of Mary, mother of Jesus.
(Luke 1:5, 36 & 59/60)
Another was Zechariah a prophet in the sixth century B.C.
(Zechariah 1:1)
And the third was a king of Israel in the eighth century B.C.,
the last of the descendents of king Jehu to be king of Israel.
(II Kings 14:29, 15:8/12 & 10:30)

546
What events of the Old Testament have the Jews survived?
The children of Israel were persecuted,
tortured, enslaved, and exiled
by the Egyptians, the Assyrians, the Babylonians,
the Medes and the Persians, the Greeks, and the Romans.
The famine of Canaan did not starve them,
their bondage and slavery in Egypt did not break them,
the waters of the Red Sea or the Jordan River
did not drown them,
the inhabitors of Canaan did not withstand them
or prevent them from rebuilding Jerusalem,
the fires of Nebuchadnezzar's furnace did not burn them,
nor did the gallows of Haman hang them.

547
Where in the Bible are seraphims mentioned?

Seraphims are angels who continuously worship God.
Seraphims are fiery angelic beings
mentioned only twice in the Bible in the commissioning of Isaiah.
"In the year that king Uzziah died I [Isaiah] saw also the Lord
sitting upon a throne, high and lifted up,
and his train filled the temple.
Above it stood the seraphims: each one had six wings;
with twain he covered his face,
and with twain he covered his feet,
and with twain he did fly.
And one cried unto another, and said, Holy, holy, holy,
is the Lord of hosts: the whole earth is full of his glory.
And the posts of the door moved at the voice of him that cried,
and the house was filled with smoke.
Then said I, Woe is me! for I am undone;
because I am a man of unclean lips,
and I dwell in the midst of a people of unclean lips:
for mine eyes have seen the King, the Lord of hosts.
Then flew one of the seraphims unto me,
having a live coal in his hand,
which he had taken with tongs from off the altar:
And he laid it upon my mouth, and said, Lo,
this hath touched thy lips;
and thine iniquity is taken away,
and thy sin purged.
And I heard the voice of the Lord, saying,
Whom shall I send, and who will go for us?
Then said I, Here am I; send me.
And he said, Go, and tell this people,
Hear ye indeed, but understand not;
and see ye indeed, but perceive not."
(Isaiah 6:1/9)

548
What were the major Gentile powers before Babylon?
The major Gentile powers before Babylon
were Egypt and Assyria.

549
Where in the Bible are cherubim mentioned?
Cherubim are mentioned 57 times in the Bible
from Genesis through Hebrews, and by reference in Revelation.
Cherubims are angelic beings
associated with the worship and praise of God.
They magnify the holiness and power of God.
(Genesis 3:24, Exodus 25:18/20 & 22, 26:1 & 31, 36:8 & 35, 37:7/9,
Numbers 7:89, I Samuel 4:4, II Samuel 6:2,
I Kings 6:23, 25, 27/29, 32 & 35, 7:29 & 36, & 8:6/7,
II Kings 19:15, I Chronicles 13:6 & 28:18,
II Chronicles 3:7, 10/11, 13/14, 5:7/8,
Psalm 80:1 & 99:1, Isaiah 37:16,
Ezekiel 10:1/3 & 5/9, 10:15/16 & 18/20 & 22, 41:18, 20 & 25,
& Hebrews 9:5)

550
What is Judaism?
Judaism is a monotheistic religion of the Jews
based on the Old Testament and the Talmud
having belief in the one God Jehovah
as creator of all things and the source of all righteousness.
Judaism rejects Jesus as the Christ
and Son of the living God,
and also rejects the Trinity
of God the Father, God the Son, and God the Holy Spirit.
Moses is the most important prophet in Judaism.
Judaism seeks salvation through God's favor,
by keeping the law, and by doing good works.

551
What is the Apocrypha?
The Apocrypha consists of fourteen biblical books
included in the Vulgate Bible, but because they are not
part of the Hebrew scriptures,
they are not considered canonical by Protestants.
Roman Catholics include eleven of the books
as canonical in the Douay Version of the Bible.

552
What are the two primary beliefs of Islam?
The two primary beliefs of Islam are:
There is no god except Allah;
and that Muhammad is the messenger of Allah.
Islam is a monotheistic religion
of one god (in one person),
as compared to Christianity
which is a monotheistic faith
of one God in three persons; God the Father, Jehovah,
and God the Son, Jesus, and God the Holy Spirit.
Jehovah and Allah are not the same god.

553
What are 'ism' religions?
'Ism' religions,
such as Hinduism, Buddhism and Secularism,
are centered around man.
"There shall be false teachers among you,
who privily shall bring in damnable heresies,
even denying the Lord that bought them,
and bring upon themselves swift destruction."
(II Peter 2:1)

554
How is T-A-O pronounced and what is it?
DOW – It is a Chinese spiritual religion of man
called 'The Way.'

555
Who were the descendents of David to Jesus?
David, Solomon, Rehoboam, Abijah, Asa, Jehoshaphat,
Jehoram, Uzziah, Jotham, Ahaz, Hezekiah,
Manasseh, Amon, Josiah, Jechoniah, Salathiel,
Zerubbabel, Abiud, Eliakim,
Azor, Sadoc, Achim, Eliud, Eleazar,
Matthan, Jacob, and
Joseph, the husband of Mary of whom was born Jesus.
(Matthew 1:6/16)

556
Who were the descendents from Adam to Mary, of whom was born Jesus?
Adam, Seth, Enos, Cainan, Maalaleel, Jared, Enoch,
Methuselah, Lamech, Noah, Sem, Arphaxad, Cainan, Salah,
Eber, Peleg, Ragau, Serug, Nahor, Terah,
Abraham, Isaac, Jacob, Judah, Pharez, Hezron, Ram,
Amminadab, Nahshon, Salmon, Boaz, Obed, Jesse, David,
Nathan, Mattatha, Menan, Melea, Eliakim, Jonan, Joseph,
Judah, Simeon, Levi, Matthat, Jorim, Eliezer, Jose, Er,
Elmodam, Cosam, Addi, Melchi, Neri, Salathiel, Zerubbabel,
Rhesa, Joanna, Judah, Joseph, Semei, Mattathias, Maath,
Naggai, Esli, Nahum, Amos, Mattathias, Joseph, Janna,
Melchi, Levi, Matthat, Heli, and Mary, of whom Jesus was born.
Heli was the father-in-law of Joseph.
(Luke 3:23/38)

557
Who were the major Bible prophets of the Old Testament in their sequence?
Isaiah, Jeremiah, Ezekiel & Daniel.
Jeremiah was the prophet in Lamentations.

558
Who were the minor Bible prophets in their Bible order?
Hosea, Joel, Amos, Obadiah,
Jonah, Micah, Nahum, Habakkuk,
Zephaniah, Haggai, Zechariah & Malachi.

559
How many years were the children of Israel
ruled by a king?
490 Years -- 1095 B.C - 605 B.C.
The children of Israel demanded a king. -- I Samuel 8:5
Saul became king in 1095 B.C.
Babylonian took control of Jerusalem in 605 B.C.

Some Bible scholars say that Israel's rebellion against God
for this 490 years is the reason that
490 years were "determined upon thy people [the children of Israel]
and upon the holy city [Jerusalem]." -- Daniel 9:24
Leviticus tells us that
"The Lord spake unto Moses in mount Sinai, saying,
Speak unto the children of Israel,
and say unto them,
When ye come into the land which I gave you,
then shall the land keep a sabbath unto the Lord.
Six years thou shalt sow thy fields,
and six years thou shalt prune thy vineyard,
and gather in the fruit thereof;
But in the seventh year shall be a sabbath
of rest unto the land,
a sabbath for the Lord:
thou shalt neither sow thy field, nor prune thy vineyard."
(Leviticus 25:1/4)
This sabbatical year was called a Shemittah [Shmita].
There were 70 Shemittah years
from 1095 B.C. to 605 B.C.

560
What are the seven Jewish Old Testament Feasts?
The seven Jewish Old Testament Feasts are:
the Feast of Unleavened Bread
(Exodus 10:2, 12:8/14 & 23:15 & Leviticus 23:5),
the Feast of Weeks
(Exodus 23:16 & 34:22 & Numbers 28:26),
the Feast of Tabernacles
(Exodus 23:16 & 34:22, Leviticus 23:34 & Deuteronomy 16:13),
the Sabbath
(Leviticus 23:2/3),
the Day of Blowing the Trumpets
(Numbers 29:1),
the Day of Atonement
(Leviticus 23:26/31),
and the Feast of Purim
(Esther 9).

561
What are the general messages of the minor Bible prophets?
Hosea – God loves Israel and wants her to repent of sin.
Joel – Judgment shall come upon Israel's sin.
Amos – A just God must judge sin.
Obadiah – Holiness shall triumph over sin.
Jonah – God's mercy is availably to the undeserving.
Micah – Christ Jesus is mankind's only deliverer.
Nahum – God's wrath is determined on wicked Nineveh.
Habakkuk – God's majestic glory shall prevail over evil.
Zephaniah – The wrath of God looms large.
Haggai – The Lord will empower the rebuilding of the temple.
Zechariah – The Lord shall not forget His people Israel.
Malachi – Israel must be obedient to God's covenant.

562
What is the most evangelistic book of the Old Testament?
The Book of Jonah
reflects the evangelistic spirit
of the New Testament better than
any other Old Testament Book.
It is a strong call for Israel,
with Jonah representing Israel,
to spread the message of God's love and forgiveness
to the Gentile nations.
(Jonah 1:2)
The Book of Jonah is to the Old Testament
what the Book of Acts is to the New Testament.

563
'The Lord giveth, and the Lord taketh away.'
Is this a quote from the Bible?
No. This is a misquote
and an incorrect preliminary conclusion of Job in Job 1:21.
We are robbed of our blessings by men and by Satan.
And we fail through disobedience
to receive all of God's blessings,
but the Lord does not take away the good and righteous things
He has given His children to enjoy.

564
'What goes around comes around.'
Is this a quote from the Bible?
No. This is a proverb, but not from the Bible.

565
What is the theological doctrine of salvation
as effected by Jesus Christ?
The theological doctrine of salvation
as effected by Jesus Christ is soterilogy.

566

What are seven things the Lord hates?
"These six things doth the Lord hate;
yea,
seven are an abomination unto him:
a proud look,
a lying tongue,
and hands that shed innocent blood,
a heart that deviseth wicked imaginations,
feet that be swift in running to mischief,
a false witness that speaketh lies,
and he that soweth discord among brethren."
(Proverbs 6:16/18)

567

Why are only certain countries and nations mentioned in the Bible?
Only countries and nations which go against the Jews
are mentioned in the Bible.

568

Which major prophet authored two books of the Old Testament, and what are the two books?
Jeremiah authored the Book of Jeremiah
and the Book of Lamentations.

569

What is the message of the Book of Ecclesiastes?
To fear God
because life lived apart from God is vanity.
(Ecclesiastes 8:12/13, & 12:13/14)
Solomon's conclusion is that God is good (2:24 & 3:13),
that God's plan is wise (3:11 & 14, 7:14 & 8:17),
and that God is just (3:17, & 8:11/13).

570
**If there were a Book of David in the Bible,
which book would it be?**
The Book of Second Samuel.

571
**Why is the Book of Ruth placed between
the Book of Judges and the Books of Samuel?**
It gives the ancestry of King David.

572
From which tribe of Israel was King Saul born?
Saul was from the tribe of Benjamin.

573
From which tribe of Israel was King David born?
David was from the tribe of Judah.
The Lord Jesus Christ is
"the Lion of the tribe of Judah,
the Root of David."
(Revelation 5:5)

574
Where did God provide a place for the solitary or the lonely?
"God setteth the solitary in the families."
(Psalm 68:6)

575
For what two women are books of the Bible named?
Ruth and Esther are the two women
for whom books of the Bible are named,
and both are books of romance.

576
Who and why are the three examples of apostates
in the Book of Jude?
Cain denied he was a sinner,
Balaam thought Israel must be judged,
and Korah contradicted the authority of Moses.
(Genesis 4:9 & Numbers 16:1/3 & 31:16)

577
Which of the Ten Commandments is not restated
in the New Testament?
Number Four - Remember the Sabbath day, to keep it holy.

578
What are the parallels between
the Bible and the Book of Isaiah?
The Bible has sixty-six books;
the Book of Isaiah has sixty-six chapters.
The Bible has thirty-nine books in the Old Testament
and twenty-seven books in the New Testament;
The first thirty-nine chapters of the Book of Isaiah
are about the law;
and the last twenty-seven chapters are about God's grace.

579
What is the center of the Bible?
Psalm 118 is the center chapter of the Bible.
There are 594 chapters before and 594 chapters after Psalm 118.
(594 + 594 = 1188 or 118:8)
"It is better to trust in the Lord than to put confidence in man."

580
What are the shortest and longest chapters of the Bible?
They are the chapters before and after Psalm 118.
Psalm 117 has two verses and is the shortest chapter of the Bible.
Psalm 119 has 176 verses and is the longest chapter of the Bible.

581
What is known as the 'Old Hundredth?'
A hymn now associated with the 100th Psalm.
Originally associated with Psalm 134,
the lyrics were:
"You faithful servants of the Lord,
sing out his praises with one accord,
while serving him with all your might
and keeping vigil through the night.
Unto his house lift up your hand
and to the Lord your praises send.
May God who made the earth and sky
bestow his blessings from on high."
and later:
"All people that on earth do dwell,
Sing to the Lord with cheerful voice.
Him serve with fear, His praise forth tell;
Come ye before Him and rejoice."
and today the lyrics are:
"Praise God, from Whom all blessings flow;
Praise Him, all creatures here below;
Praise Him above, ye heavenly host;
Praise Father, Son, and Holy Ghost."
Commonly known today as 'The Doxology.'

582
What happened to the tabernacle at Shiloh?
Later, when the children of Israel provoked God to anger
with their high places and graven images,
God forsook the tabernacle of Shiloh.
(Psalm 78:60)

583
**What is the difference between a Shemittah year
and a year of Jubilee?**
A Shemittah (Shmita) year is the seventh year
of the seven-year agricultural cycle.
(Leviticus 25:4/7)
God required sabbatical years for the children and Land of Israel.
(Exodus 23:11)
Debts owed by other children of Israel
are to be released at the end of a shemittah year.
(Deuteronomy 15:1/6)
After seven sabbaths, or after forty-nine years,
the fiftieth year shall be a year of Jubilee
in which land is to returned
to the original owners or heirs
and slaves are to be returned to their families.
as prescribed in the Book of Leviticus.
(Leviticus 25:8/10)
A year of Jubilee is also to be as a sabbatical year
for the Land of Israel.
(Leviticus 25:11)

584
What is a way that a wicked man can be discerned?
"A wicked doer giveth heed to false lips;
and a liar giveth ear to a naughty tongue."
(Proverbs 17:4)

585
What does a fool say in his heart?
"The fool hath said in his heart, There is no God."
(Psalm 14:1)
But God said, "I am the Lord, and there is none else,
there is no God beside me."
(Isaiah 45:5)

586
Why did God send judgment upon Israel?

The reason God judged Israel is recapped in the 78th Psalm.
"They remembered not [God's] hand,
nor the day when he delivered them from the enemy.
How [God] had wrought his signs in Egypt,
and his wonders in the field of Zoan
[which was an ancient city of Egypt]:
And had turned their rivers into blood;
and their floods, that they could not drink.
He sent [various] sorts of flies among them, which devoured them;
and frogs, which destroyed them.
He gave also their increase unto the caterpillar,
and their labor unto the locust.
He destroyed their vines with hail,
and their sycamore [or fig] trees with frost.
He gave up their cattle also to the hail,
and their flocks to hot thunderbolts.
He cast upon them the fierceness
of his anger, wrath, and indignation, and trouble,
by sending evil angels among them.
He made a way to his anger;
he spared not their soul from death,
but gave their life over to pestilence;
And smote all the first-born in Egypt;
the chief of their strength in the tabernacles of Ham:
But made his own people to go forth like sheep,
and guided them in the wilderness like a flock.
And he led them on safely, so that they feared not:
but the sea overwhelmed their enemies.
And he brought them to the border of his sanctuary,
even to this mountain [of Moriah],
which his right hand had purchased.
He cast out the heathen also before them,
and divided them an inheritance by line,
and made the tribes of Israel to dwell in their tents.

Yet they tempted and provoked the most high God,
and kept not his testimonies:
"But turned back, and dealt unfaithfully like their fathers:
they were turned aside like a deceitful bow.
For they provoked [God] to anger
with their high places [to worship false gods],
and moved him to jealousy with their graven images."
(Psalm 78:42/58)
Israel did not exist as a nation for more than 2,500 years.

587
Why did God uproot the nation of Israel?
Israel did not exist as a nation from 605 B.C. until May 15, 1948
because "They [Israel] remembered not [God's] hand,
nor the day when he delivered them from the enemy.
How [God] had wrought his signs in Egypt,
and his wonders in the field of Zoan
[which was an ancient city of Egypt]:
And had turned their rivers into blood;
and their floods, that they could not drink.
He sent [various] sorts of flies among them,
which devoured them;
and frogs, which destroyed them.
He gave also their increase unto the caterpillar,
and their labor unto the locust.
He destroyed their vines with hail,
and their sycamore [or fig] trees with frost.
He gave up their cattle also to the hail,
and their flocks to hot thunderbolts.
He cast upon them the fierceness
of his anger, wrath, and indignation, and trouble,
by sending evil angels among them.
He made a way to his anger;
he spared not their soul from death,
but gave their life over to pestilence;

And smote all the first-born in Egypt;
the chief of their strength in the tabernacles of Ham:
But made his own people to go forth like sheep,
and guided them in the wilderness like a flock.
And he led them on safely,
so that they feared not:
but the sea overwhelmed their enemies.
And he brought them to the border of his sanctuary,
even to this mountain [of Moriah],
which his right hand had purchased.
He cast out the heathen also before them,
and divided them an inheritance by line,
and made the tribes of Israel to dwell in their tents.
Yet they tempted and provoked the most high God,
and kept not his testimonies:
But [Israel] turned back, and dealt unfaithfully
like their fathers:
they were turned aside like a deceitful bow.
For they provoked [God] to anger
with their high places [to worship false gods],
and moved [God] to jealousy
with their graven images."
(Psalm 78:42/58)

588
What does the sabbath celebrate?
The sabbath or seventh day of the week
celebrates the creation of God.
"On the seventh day God ended his work which he had made;
and he rested on the seventh day
from all his work which he had made.
And God blessed the seventh day, and sanctified it
[or set it aside]:
because that in it he had rested from all his work
which God created and made."
(Genesis 2:2/3)

589

**Why do Christians celebrate the first day of the week
instead of the seventh day of the week?**
Because the resurrection of Jesus Christ from the dead
on the first day of the week represents a new beginning.
Creation was spoiled by the sin of Adam.
Jesus came to pay the penalty of sin,
to overcome world and destroy death,
and to redeem "whosoever believeth in him."
(Matthew 28:1/6, John 16:33, I Corinthians 15:26 & John 3:15/16)

590

**Why did Jesus cry out loud from the cross,
"My God, my God, Why hast thou forsaken me?**
Jesus was drawing attention to the 22nd Psalm
to explain what was happening.
Jesus had been rejected as the Christ and the Son of God,
and he was paying the penalty of death
which was the price of redemption.
The Old Testament was without chapters and verses
as it is today.
A scripture passage was referenced
by quoting the first sentence or words of the passage.

Question

_____

_____

_____**?**

Answer

_____

_____

_____

_____

_____

_____

_____

_____**.**

(_____)

Question

_____

_____

_____**?**

Answer

_____

_____

_____

_____

_____

_____

_____

_____**.**

(_____)

May the grace of our Lord Jesus Christ be with you all.
Amen.

(Revelation 22:21)

ABOUT THE AUTHOR

Jerry Adams is a member of a Southern Baptist Convention member church and a Bible student and teacher. He teaches Jesus Christ crucified and resurrected and coming again as King of kings and as Lord of lords.

His faith and his trust and his hope are in Jesus, the Christ and Son of the living God, and the only way to salvation by virtue of God's grace. Jerry has been born again in the Spirit.

He believes in God the Father, God the Son, and God the Holy Spirit as one God in three persons. He believes that God created man, the world and all things.

He believes that "God so loved the world, that he gave his only begotten Son [Jesus Christ], that whosoever believeth in him should not perish, but have everlasting life." (John 3:16)

He believes that Christians are believers who have been saved by faith unto good works, and that good works based on loving God and loving others are evidence of true faith.

And he believes that the resurrection of Jesus Christ from death back to life, never to die again, is proof of the promise of a future resurrection of all men and a coming day of judgment – a judgment of works for believers and a judgment of damnation for nonbelievers. Jesus said, "He that believeth and is baptized [by the Holy Spirit] shall be saved; but he that believeth not shall be damned." (Mark 16:16)

Jerry believes in dispensational theology and in the restoration of Israel, with Jerusalem as the future capital of the Millennial kingdom of Jesus Christ.

He is watching for the rapture of believers by Jesus Christ, and believes that it will be followed by a seven-year period of tribulation on earth and then a return to this earth by Jesus Christ with all the saints to reign for a thousand years before this world passes away and all things are made new. (II Peter 3:10 & 13)

His non-published works include an Expounding Christianity series and a Prophecy series which he has distributed to class participants, family members and others.

Jerry married his high school girlfriend in 1965 after graduating from college. They have two children, four grandchildren and a great grandchild.

In 1971, Jerry co-founded a CPA firm, which with God's blessing, soon became a top 100 firm in the profession. He was managing partner of the firm for thirty years, became the firm's senior partner, and continues to practices as a CPA.